From Incontinence to Injustice

by Greck

RoseDog Books
585 Alpha Drive
Pittsburgh, PA 15222
Visit our website at www.rosedogbookstore.com
Order toll free 1-800-788-7654 United States

ISBN: 978-1-4809-7201-8
eISBN 978-1-4809-7178-3

From Incontinence to Injustice
An Introduction

The first 24 chapters, were finished 2 years ago, but although I sent it to several publishers, they were either not interested in the contents, suggested I got a ghost writer, explained they only deal via agents, but refused to say who their agents are et etcetera.

I then sent some copies to friends and one of them replied, that although he found most of it interesting, I should remove the part about being sent to prison, as everyone in the legal profession would know it was a pure fantasy on my part... I had forgotten he was a retired barrister, but just the same pointed out, it was not a fantasy on my part.

Then asked if I could be arrested for pointing out the facts of my trial, even though not directly asking to go to the Court of Appeal...due to my conditions of discharge.

He again, pointed out that I should erase the part about the trial and repeated why, adding that after all the years he has known me, he never once had reason to question my truth, but now he was in doubt about other things I have said about other things over the years we had known each other.

Maybe at this rate it will never be printed in my life time, but hopefully one day I will discover a way around it and hopefully a lot of those publishers will be overjoyed at the knowledge that had they bothered to read it, several hundreds, if not thousands of children would not have died needlessly.

This part of the book is in many ways strange, but then not much stranger than the rest of my life, but at least I have a lot more facts on my trial than I had before.

But yet again it was suggested I rewrite the parts about the trial as I remembered it, all those years ago [I don't know if I have already pointed out that I have a retentive memory, of things that have actually happened, but a completely lousy memory for people's names] but I refused yet again to do as requested, which proved a good thing, otherwise I wouldn't have obtained all the extra information, needed to prove my story.

I have also acquired the name of the detective who it proves was a complete liar and framed me, although that too was suggested, not to imply he framed me, in case he is still alive…

I really hope he is still alive and this is published in his life time, because I really hope he will die a very miserable and lonely death, as his family and friends will reject him, for the sick bastard he really is and hopefully every parent whose child was murdered will send him hate mail for the rest of his life, because in framing me, he condoned the murder of that child and let someone else go free to kill another child with his blessings and greed for promotion, with 30 pieces of brass to add to his income/pay rise.

2 Eventually my friendly barrister accepted that I was not going to remove that part of my history, and to prove he was right that I imagined the whole thing, suggested that I wrote to the Court Archives, where I was sentenced for a copy of the depositions, but they replied that they had never heard of me or a trial taking place during that period!

Which cheered him up no end, as it was all the proof he needed, but again I insisted, the trial had taken place and after an argument he gave me another address to write to and got another negative reply, pointing out they had no record of it taking place at any Crown Courts, Sessions or Quarter Sessions.

It did not matter where I wrote…the replies were always the same, hence he told me again to erase my fantasy trial and consequence…

Although in many ways I wish I had listened, because then I would not have discovered also just how evil my daughter is, plus carried on with my normal life, having had the operation and enjoying a new found freedom going anywhere I pleased, but it was a case of Pride and Proving I was not a Liar, talk….about Pride before the Fall or in this case; The Fool!

Oh a digression is needed here, I had met him not long after being discharged, as he was ask to represent me at a case where someone had set fire to the women's toilet in the factory, where I was on the night shift…I found myself being arrested and charged with arson, because when I heard where the fire was I could not contain my mirth and started singing, that old music hall song; "Please don't burn our shithouse down, mother is willing to pay!" One of the side effects of smoking pot an hour or so earlier.

Which was a lot more reason, I suppose to be arrested than for the charge of murder, where my only guilt was being in the area, sometime before or after the murder took place, which they decided was the time of death, also it was claimed I was the last person to see the kid, well as no one else admitted seeing the child after I did, so apparently being the last to acknowledge seeing him alive, was enough to charge me with murder, overlooking the murderer was hardly going to admit to seeing or being with him.

Plus I now have some official statements that are protected under "The Official Secrets Act" and could have remained as secrets, which implied that the fact I still wet the bed at 16, made me the most probable candidate likely to commit the crime, being amongst other things "An Inadequate Psychopath!"

How's that for a solution to all our serious crimes, sort out everyone who is incapable of being a psychopath and look them away, to protect society.

When I was in Broadmoor I was labelled as an; "Intellectual Eccentric", some-one who is unlikely to become a genius, but equally unlikely to become a mad-man…in other words an "Inadequate Psychopath!"

Yet I digress: I will explain if possible such stupidity!"

Oh before going on, here is a digression worthy of a digression, when the person read the book, he noted the name Paddy Lester and wrote to her, at Southend General Hospital, to discover she was the person he knew years ago at college and had been her husband's best man at their wedding.

Now that could be said to add to the notion of; "It's a Small World."

Although whenever I went to Heathrow Airport, to reduce the waiting time boredom, I would approach strangers and exclaim; "Isn't it a Big World, I have never seen you before!" This resulted in either blank faces or good laughs as it occurred to them what I had said…then we'd chat about all those stupid Hollywood Movies etc.,

It's a bit like all those well-dressed people looking disdainfully at hippies, then I would try to make polite conversation with them…only to be treated with con-tempt, then choosing that moment to point out; that I am completely naked under all my clothing, which really upset them and they became genuinely disgusted… but sometimes the penny dropped and they would either smile or laugh and a chat about reality.

But then I had a good friend called Tim Smith who worked with the deaf and pointed out what they were saying about us, then as either they or us were about to walk away, he would tell them he was a lip-reader…so sometimes when it was ob-vious people were not only glaring at me but attracting more attention to me, I would also walk over to them and say exactly the same thing…sadly working with the deaf is something I regretfully never got into, especially when seeing people saying goodbyes from a train without the windows open, but still from time to time drop my imaginary bomb-shell.

Oh as I was saying, because I had no evidence he implied [Ron Trott that is] it all sounded a bit farfetched and still thought I had made it all up, about being charged with murder and spending 15 years in prisons and other institutions, a bit like the disbelieving Probation Officer who made the telling of my story more possible.

Well as everyone knows; Britain has a system whereby whenever a miscarriage of justice takes place in the Commonwealth, it gets on its high horse and condemns dictators as being inhumane…Our Prime Ministers must get into office via some really dubious routes, if they have no idea, that this country has more guilt on its shoulders, than most countries, when it comes to threatening innocent people with reimprisonment, if they seek for the Truth on discharge…

It is now 1996 and there is some poor sod, who has spent 23 years in prison, for a crime he claims he has not committed, the Home Office is refusing to review his case until he admits his guilt, but he will probably end up in Broadmoor one day, because it stands to reason, that anyone in England who cannot accept they are guilty of not being guilty, must be psychologically disturbed, because no one has been convicted in this Country of a crime they have not committed, everyone with half a brain Knows that Everyone is Innocent, until Proved Insane enough to believe in British Justice.

Insanity being another word for Innocent…i.e. we all use the term Innocent as a Baby, but throughout t book one it has been explained with quotes by unquestionable experts in child psychology, that all children are psychologically sexually disturbed; especially if they wet the bed, then it's because they want sex with both of their parents, but if they don't wet the bed then it's because of the Electra or Oedipus complexes that cause boys to want to murder their father's so they can marry their mothers and the reverse for girls, who are even more disturbed, because they want to kill their mothers, so they can marry their dead fathers.

Regardless of the fact that Oedipus didn't kill his father, to marry his mother and Electra's father had already been murdered by her mother, before she and her brother killed their mother and her mother's lover, plus not overlooking that silly little detail, that neither Oedipus or Electra ever existed outside the mind of Sophocles.

Yet in the dying years of the 20th century, these theories are still being used to create, our own "Unquestionable Justice System!

It was only after visiting a friend, who put on the film 1984…something to do with a project he was working on…well in the main I found it a bit boring, but all the way home something kept nagging me about the film, but for the life of me, I couldn't say what or why, hence early the next morning, I popped in to ask if he still had the film, then asked to watch it again [not putting it off that it may not have been all that important or the fact what I saw had only conjured up a memory of something else] then an easy to overlook detail came on the screen, but only for a few seconds…oh the film centered around causing someone to completely disappear and destroying any evidence he ever existed, those brief moments show a guy cutting out items in a newspaper and a big smile spread across my face and just hoped that Big Brother had overlooked, destroying all the old news items of the period.

Hence I visited the BML [British Museum Library] got my dates wrong and had to wait another 3 hours for the right paper and there it was; "My Trial!"

Got a few photocopies, that are not cheap from them, then made extra copies in a local shop and sent them off to my friendly QC…then as if the Fates were smiling gently on me, I was sent an offer from National Express to visit anywhere in the country for £5…so off I Jolly well went to Carlisle, returning home with a pile of photocopies, plus a nice long walk in Penrith, to recapture an almost forgotten memory of going there whilst at the Approved school back in 1960.

Well something came into my mind, that maybe the Home Office, was just pretending to be Big Brother, having overlooked to destroy all the old newspapers, where I found a few references to my trial, very bias articles, but evidence in themselves.

So I sent them off to him and a long correspondence began, well having his office in the Temple Court, he knew quite a few people and decided to take my case on, as a conclusion before retirement.

He made some interesting discoveries, such as my case was under the Official Secrets Act…which cheered a few of my friends up, knowing an official secret i.e. Myself or maybe all my friends are psychologically disturbed as well , suffering with a mass hysteria, that causes them all to imagine that I actually exist.

Well most official secrets are revealed to the public after 50 years, from the day they became such, in my case there is a 75 year ban from the date of conviction, which means; the public can have access to them, if or when I reach 92 years of age.

During this period I sent a letter to Sir Teddy Taylor, explaining how my medical files and probation files have disappeared, but although they were only mentioned as a digression, he approached the Parliamentary Under Secretary of State, pointing them out as the reason for my letter, instead of asking why I cannot have access to my depositions.

I will copy out the entire letter, because within it you will see, that the Home Office still had no idea, how far I had gotten and were completely unaware, I had a Barrister giving me Advice

I will point out other observations afterwards.

Official letters can sometimes be great fun to read, especially those writing them, overlook the obvious and give away too much, by trying to use deceit, as with the probation office, who gave me a lot of ammunition to prove my innocence, but then he was also unaware of the facts.

This part of this book is mainly to let you the public to reach your own conclusions, not just on my innocence, but also the guilt of those who make the laws that control us, explaining their evil away, as helping people to live in a free society with delusions of Justice Protecting Them.

Them? Sorry I mean You, the person reading this, You! Hello have I got some news for You, You can go to prison if you carry on reading this book, because you will be guilty of subversion, being aware of an Official Secret or two. How does it feel? I bet you are wearing a smile, which is just as cynical as my own.

The letter sent to Sir Teddy Taylor and passed on to me, which is a common practice, well known by all parties, that a copy of whatever they write may end up in the original enquirers hands…a point I will touch on later.

Sent by the Parliamentary Under Secretary of State, Home Office, Queen Anne's Gate, London, SW1H 9AT, dated 18.4.95. Reference number/s; Our Ref; CR1/95 189/3/91 PO 05377/95.

Dear Teddy,

Thank you for your letter of 12 March to Michael Howard when you enclosed this one from Mr M Greck who, under the name of Malcolm Peck, was found guilty of manslaughter on the grounds of diminished responsibility in 1961. He was sentenced to life imprisonment and began his sentence at Wakefield Prison. However, in October 1971, Mr Peck was transferred to Broadmoor and in January 1975 again transferred to Runwell Hospital from where he was conditionally discharged in June 1976. Under the terms of this discharge he was required, inter alia, to report to a supervising probation officer. He was therefore supervised by Essex Probation and After-Care for almost five years from the time of discharge.

On 2 February 1982 Home Office officials wrote to Mr Peck to inform him that the Home Secretary had decided that the conditions attached to his discharge were being allowed to elapse. This meant that he would no longer obliged to reside at a specified address, be supervised by the probation services or attend an out-patient clinic. However, as he is aware, he remains liable to be recalled to hospital for further treatment should the need ever arise.

Mr Greck is concerned about the fact his prison records are not available for inspection. I can assure you that there is nothing untoward about the way his records have been handled. His representative was apparently informed that his records had been closed from public inspection for 50 years; this is by no means uncommon with prisoners personal files as they often contain medical and welfare reports which have been written in confidence and could not be opened for inspection without compromising the confidentiality of both the author and the subject.

Generally speaking, such papers are held in the Department until they are no longer needed for administrative purposes. A decision is then made as to whether they are of sufficient historical importance to warrant retention in the Public Records Office. Very few fall into this category, the remainder are destroyed. I can confirm that our records show that the Prison Commission's file on Mr Greck was destroyed as part of this standard procedure in 1988.

Mr Greck refers also to the question of appeal against his conviction in 1961. As you know, the legal remedy open to anyone dissatisfied with the decision of the court in his case is to appeal to a higher one. In Mr Greck's case this would be the Court of Appeal (Criminal Division).

Notice of appeal should normally be given within 28 days of the conviction, but it may be given later with the leave of the Court. However, it is entirely a matter for Mr Greck to decide whether or not to seek leave to appeal out of time and this letter should not be taken as advising him in any way.

In view of the fact that the early files have been destroyed I am afraid that I am unable to comment on Mr Greck's allegation that, two years after being sentenced , the Home Office had proof that Mr Greck was not guilty of the crime of which he had been convicted. Files we do have, dating from the mid-1970's and relating to his conditional discharge from hospital, do not support this allegation however.

In these circumstances it may be helpful to you and Mr Greck if I explain something of the Home Secretary's powers to respond to allegations that there has been a miscarriage of justice. In accordance with section 17 of the Criminal Appeal Act 1968, the Home Secretary can refer to the Court of Appeal the case of a person who has been convicted on indictment.

It is, however, a basic principle of our system of justice that the decisions of the courts are free from interference by the Government. The Home Secretary would not therefore, consider taking action unless there has been some new evidence or other consideration of substance which had not been before the court and which appeared to cast some doubt on the safety of the conviction. I have to say, moreover, that the Home Secretary will not normally consider taking action unless a person's right to appeal has been exhausted, although in some cases. It maybe that the best course of action would be for Mr Greck to consult a solicitor as to his prospects for a successful appeal, or for finding fresh evidence or argument upon which representations for the referral of a conviction could be based.

I hope this is helpful
Nickolas Baker.

*   *   *   *   *

I suppose I should start this section, by saying an ineffable Thank You to Nicky Baker, for being so confident, that he told me a lot of information I had not exactly asked for, whilst avoiding the exact questions, in the letter to Sir Teddy Taylor... without realizing I needed his deceptions to support my story and wow how on earth can a person be expected to put so much official crap in one letter?

I thought it was only the general public that was being taken for a ride, now we know the Cabinet Ministers take the Back Benchers for a ride as well.

Oh the punctuation in the letter was recorded faithfully.

So once again we are left to ask...Just who is running this country, if not those we vote in to protect us, who for the most part are given a load of crap to pass on to the electorate or should that be: "illiterate" who think they are intelligent, because illiterate usually means someone who cannot read and write or do maths but in this case it means someone who cannot read between the line, not because the print is so fine, but it's in a secret code known only to Government Freemason's.

To the letter, why was it deemed necessary to point out I had changed my name and had been in Broadmoor?

Because I had already explained all those things to Sir Teddy, as they were common knowledge…well a lot of people know these facts by being told by me, although they had nothing to do with my depositions, the crap about destroying non historically interesting papers, was all that would have been needed to explain…

Or was he saying: Well think about it Teddy, anyone who has been in Broadmoor is obviously a few Civil Servants short of a corrupted system nudge, nudge say no more!"

Well at least I discovered something new, I was also under the supervision of the After-Care Services, who are those people? Some secret society that goes around supervising people without telling them, until only after they stop supervising them, just think over those 5 years we could have become quite good friends, not only that, but they may have been able to give me some assistance in adapting to society, as their impressive sounding name implies, they just may have been in the habit of doing.

Then as already explained earlier in the other book, he implies that after five years, it was decided I didn't have to report to anyone any more, which as I have also stated , it's a great system we have, where most ex-lifers have to report for the rest of their lives, but those classified as psychopaths as well as psychologically disturbed in various forms, that have been committed to Broadmoor, are allowed to roam around freely unobserved, especially those who have a strange illness that will only manifest itself, when the Home Office decides it's time for such a state of mind to exist…being returned to hospital if the need ever arises.

Note I was discharged in 1976…and this letter was written in 1995…19 years later and still this mysterious ailment has not shown itself, what on earth repeats itself after 19 years, it's a wonder anyone ever managed to track down such a disorder, well we only know to date it doesn't happen after 19 years, so could it take place every 25 years!

Now who was under observation for that length of time, for their psychologist to observe their patient had done exactly the same thing 25 years earlier and again 25 years later…the guy must have been over 100 years old, before the observations lapsed or came to a standstill.

Cynical? Who Me? Never! I just find something's that are said by extremely intelligent people, who may well be well-versed in the postulations of psychology very hard not to laugh at, because it is obvious they have got to be joking, no one should be able to accept that much comedy, without laughing themselves stupid enough to be a perfect candidate for observation.

In the next paragraph, note how a reference is made to my representative, they had no idea about who was helping me, knew a great deal about the law and had already tracked down my files from the Home Office and were being held under "SS" (4) of the Public Records Act 1967, at which the Keeper of Public Records may permit inspection notwithstanding the Public Records Act 1958 on the special authority of an officer of a government department or other body who is accepted by the Lord Chancellor as qualified to give that authority.

I already knew this because it is a quote from a letter, sent to me on 3.11.94. Five months before the one above…The Home Office obviously had no idea what was going on, how much I knew and in knowing, be able to read this letter between the lines and see the obvious lies, that I am pointing out to the world, who will have to be very foolish…i.e. married to a government minister who has declared he has never worn her underwear or slept with anyone else, note not just another woman, but anyone else from a shirt lifting public school.

Nicky then goes on to say; it is not uncommon for records to be closed for 50 years…to protect the ranting's , lies and falsifying of evidence, performed by those freaks who control society and destroy people's lives, whilst never having to justify their theories, reassured that their psychologically disturbed secrets, will only be revealed after they die.

What sort of sickness, brought about such a law into a civilized society?

Yeah You've guessed it…somewhere later in this chapter or the next, I will be quoting their depraved minds and at times word for word, some of which would have been extremely funny, except for what they brought about in my life, and who will know how many other people's lives these freaks destroyed, in the knowledge that British Justice will protect them for the rest of their pathetic lives!

Let's go on into the letter, generally speaking, any file that is not of sufficient historical importance are destroyed; it's a standard procedure, well maybe it is, who am I to suggest otherwise, just think how cluttered up the Home Office would be, if they kept those files for 50 years, when the public would be able to read them [especially those of innocent people who committed suicide, whilst stripped off naked in padded cells], because they are not of any historical value, unlike the Dandy or Beano, which are not only in the BML, but on microfilm as well, which seems to imply The Home Office is so far out of touch with reality, that it closes its eyes to the fact that almost every 20th century reference library has a microfilm or fish eye department, that can contain the entire volumes of The Encyclopedia Britannica!

Yet the Home Office seems to be implying it doesn't have access to such technology or can it be we detect a slight digression from the facts.

Covering the procedure of appealing, note the last sentence that the matter is in my hands, but this letter should not be taken as offering advice in any way.

On the surface that sounds pretty innocent, but who was he addressing Teddy or me?

It has been obvious in a few places the letter was being written directly to me, the only flaw in my earlier chapter, was that I thought the period of appeal was 6 weeks , but it turns out to be four weeks...but then I was pretty confused at the time, what with the shock of being found guilty, convinced innocent people, could never be found guilty under British Justice, but whatever the time period was , it was also just enough time for a court appointed solicitor to fall off the planet or kept distracted so much they forget, their last victim was really in need of their advice and guidance, but hey that's British Justice for you.

In the next part we have a great if not classic observation; because the files were "Destroyed" there is no evidence left to confirm the Home Office had any proof, I had not committed the crime...

My friend did make a small observation as we were sharing my copy of another letter, where my blood group came up, because not long after going to prison I joined the National Blood Transfusion [regardless of my dread of needles] and on my card with my blood group on it, which is not exactly the communal garden variety, that although an A group, it will destroy all the evidence against me and still will, unless like my files anything with possible DNA evidence , will have also been destroyed.

Notice how my files only go back as far as just before I was discharged, how very convenient, considering it's of no historical importance, so why keep it, but it would be interesting to know exactly what I wrote in my "encouraged confession" [after having spent 28 years in institutions and still only 32 years old] all I can recall of it, was I had written several tongue in cheek statements, using psychology and gave them the funniest one first...and surprisingly they accepted it, but then they were psychologist and nothing destroys psychology, easier than another postulation of psychology, but I do know it was not a confession as such...that would stand up in a court.

Another point to take into consideration, about the file from the mid-70's, is why did they bother to keep such a file, because before they destroyed the prison and medical files. I had already had all my conditions of discharge removed in 1988 [according to them in this letter]...double back to the full letter...

"Second paragraph...On 2 February 1982 the Home Office officials wrote to Mr Peck to inform him..."

…that after 6 years all my conditions elapsed, now considering I was given a complete discharge in June 1976…now I appreciate I am fairly useless at maths, but this letter was sent in 1995, which implies they have kept one hell of a lot of information of no historical importance…because I am sure, his memory for dates, especially those he had hitherto never heard of and worse still comes that horrendous reality that in the last 50 years the only Member of Parliament who was not a compulsive liar was Sir Teddy Taylor…no wonder he was never considered for party leader or P.M.

Okay this maybe a trivial point, but also in the first 2 paragraph's he kept referring to me as Peck then in the rest of the letter Greck…but no reference to the fact they had no idea I had change my name by accident or it was myself who informed them of the error.

At least it is reassuring that the basic principles or our system of justice are free from interference from the Government, I am sure that will come as very reassuring to the mother's and families of the men that were hanged on flimsy evidence and wasted all that time writing to the Home Secretary at the Home Office, but were never informed about the "principles" of our justice system.

Plus over the years all the evidence was destroyed on the ground it had no historical interest, probably destroyed whilst the bodies were still twitching and what of those innocent victims of miscarriages of justice, that spend years in prisons and Top Security Psychiatric Hospitals, until they decline their human rights via physical or psychological torture, to implicate themselves in a crime they were never in any way involved with…with the added threat, that if they ever discover enough evidence to clear their names, they are dissuaded from doing so, because anyone seeking for the Truth in this Country is considered as having a psychological relapse!

Oh a small digression, almost everything in this book up until now, was to seek help and protection for people with severe incontinence…plus the rest of the book is to carry on along those lines, except from now on…a great deal of the information may help the general public, that they are all guilty unless they can prove otherwise and no one in H.M.Government give a toss about whether or not they will destroy your lives or those of your families…and yet they still tell us that Adolph Hitler was evil…so just who are they descendants of, apart from very conscious child molesters?

But back to the implication in this letter; which raises another interesting question, if Truth is considered as an ailment only to be found in the psychologically disturbed, then what is it, other than deceit, we are being given daily by the Government and is it also taken for granted, that if someone tells the Truth on oath, they too are suitable cases for observation?

As to having come across new evidence or other consideration of substance, what a load of bullshit, several people over the years, have discovered evidence, that should have proved conclusively that they are victims of a miscarriage of justice, which was then thrown out of the Court of Appeals, probably unread…which yet again is a subject I will be covering later.

Now for the funniest part of his letter, in which Nicky was just a little too over confident in expressing himself; when he suggested that maybe my best course of action, would be to consult a solicitor as to my prospects of finding fresh evidence or argument, on which representation for a referral of conviction could be based.

As already pointed out I had a High Court Barrister working with me, without anything but the facts [he had discovered] that my records had been destroyed and all my conditions for discharge had elapsed, after apparently five years, although I was not involved with the After-care Services and nor had the Probation Services any records of my case, except those discovered after a year of searching for them, plus the 75 years restriction of the public access to the files, when most prison files, are usually closed only for 30 years.

Now to cover a few points, having finished with the letter, which you may have returned to, to read with opened eyes…

What the Home Office failed to tell Nick, who was unaware of several things, first I was already aware of the 30 and 50 year bans [the former for public crimes and the latter for war crimes], but on my files they put a 75 year ban on public access, which meant I would have to wait until I reached 92 years of age, before the public could have official access to them, which seems to imply, someone in the Home Office definitely has something to hide….could it be The Truth or The Reality of British Justice?

Another thing he was unaware of; was that the Home Office is not the only place, copies of the statements are kept, they are also kept in the Lord Chancellors Office, needless to say this wasn't the easiest bit of information to acquire, but it's nice to have a friend, with Honest Friends in High Places!

Yet another thing he was unaware of; was that at the time he was drafting his letter to Sir Teddy, I had already been given an appointment on the 31st of March 1995, to inspect and go through all the files at The Lord Chancellors Office on 28.4.95 10 days after he wrote to Sir Teddy, so what with it going to Sir Teddy and being passed on to myself, the chances are I received the letter just a few days before going to the LCO, which gave me even more reason to laugh, about his suggestion I should consult a solicitor…who considering how long it took for a High Court Barrister and his friends, to trace the whereabouts of the documents…a solicitor would have given up…but then I suppose it must be fairly common knowledge in the Home Office, that there is no way a Joe Blogs will ever discover, that such information can be seen without going to the Home Office…

Note it was my depositions…not my prison files I was seeking for, as no other Public Records Office's had ever heard of me, yes I did write to them using both the names Peck and Greck, enclosing my Deed Poll.

Oh I seem to have missed out a big chunk of how I came to be aware of a lot of things…unless it appears somewhere else in my wanderings off subject and oh yeah the following if included, may change in a few words…but the facts of what happened will remain the same.

After having contacted all the various places of the Court Archives and came up blank, my friend was triumphant having proved himself to be right all along, because no one can pull the wool over his eyes, when it comes to the Laws of England and Wales….sometimes I wish I had left it alone with a shrug off my shoulders, such as that when an obvious guilty person is found guilty by a jury, but no, because having been the victim of so many evil people in authority, throughout my entire life, I couldn't just give up, plus had I known what the rest of my life was going to be like, I may have given up and just write the book again, just concentrating on incontinence…without historical information or inventing a fantasy to cover those years I spent in prison…snag is I am also not a novelist!

Okay getting this letter just prior to going to the LCO, did fill me with a lot of apprehension, not knowing how close or far apart communications are between those two departments are, then my friend turned up late, I was very on edge… because maybe the very fact I was seeking proof, may have been misconstrued as a violation of my discharge conditions.

We were shown into an office and given every scrap of paper to look at and take notes from, although several very important statements were missing i.e. my signed statement to the police and the statement from my most important witnesses, in fact according to the files, my witness had never given a statement to the police, then another snag…the only statements given were those that covered initial statements that the police liked, not the trial statements, but those invented by the police, who had obviously not read them, before enclosing them as evidence and from another source the press reports were very bias…but that's only to be expected, owing to the nature of the case and being unaware of the doctored police statements.

Anyway we took a lot of notes, with my friend pointing out, he had never seen such a white washed case, but on getting home, I found I had forgotten a couple of points and that others made no sense whatsoever, so I wrote again to the LCO for another appointment and was given something not expected, they had photocopied everything for me, although they were also confused at how much was missing to the files, considering the list of the items that should have been in the folder, plus one statement well the judges copy of notes, had become too faded and discoloured to photocopy…but at least some very damaging to the police statements, but I feel the Home Office felt very safe leaving in the police statements…but then it took me over a week, reading them several times a day, during which I was becoming very depressed, to discover the lies, that were very cleverly written, but then I also was given a map of the area, which confirmed my story or events, then proved almost conclusively it was a frame up and the officer in charge of the investigation, to be a compulsive liar, because he overstepped himself, once too often trying to appear to be a lot more intelligent than he was.

Plus he had not read the Coroner's report, which was written a few days later.

*   *   *   *   *

Part Two

Chapter 1
The Statements

I was going to copy out the statements, then add my comments and point out the flaws in it, but owing to the statement by the psychiatrist, that was made in the court and probably the only closely reported section in the press, what I will do is, after the first police statement, I will copy out the psychiatrist statement, then the other police statement.

The reason for this is, if I were to do them all at once, then add comments it gets confusing so adding comments at the end of each statement, then on both statements, for cross referencing.

The doctor's statement is in a league of its own, as the first I had ever known it had taken place, was when I came across references to it, in the files and read it in the press report.

Note I came across these things during March 1995 or 34 years after they were made, although I may have heard it in the court and completely forgot about it, but then who has ever heard of a psychiatrist being questioned, by anyone who may be made to look foolish or neurotic?

It can be said by anyone, especially The Home Office, that my saying this interview never took place, is on my part a delusion or I had forgotten, but as you read into it, you too will become aware it never took place.

Yes I admit there are a great many small details I had forgotten, but reading the statements, brought them all flooding back, like reading an old text book from your school days and then remembering what is on the next page or being able to conjure up old images of where you were at the time or looking at old holiday snaps for the first time in years and remembering, who is in the picture with you or where you were, plus long ago forgotten insignificant details.

First the police statement, I will point out that it has been cleverly constructed, so much so that is very probable, that the reason it is in the files, is because anyone reading it will think automatically, that it speaks for itself and an idiot will not have any problems, in seeing that the person is obviously guilty, until a little part here and there, causes an intelligent person to ask: "How on Earth did my Q.C. allow it to go unchallenged, having all the statements, plus a map of the area?"

Yet it has already been pointed out, he did not even help me with my Appeal, after telling me to do nothing until he had come to see me, had he done so, I am sure my life would have been very different and I would still be fairly illiterate, as the Home Office wouldn't have been so eager to cover up the lies of the police… and who's to say did not bring about continued sexual assaults of children or had their bodies, hidden more carefully, because I am sure the person, who killed the child did not write my number on the hanky or the number of another approved school boy, who had been at the hospital 18 months earlier, which in itself is an interesting feat, two hankies being found with the numbers of the only two boys to have been at the hospital…

Coincidence or An Extremely Convenient Coincidence?

I am sure the Judge must have had; copies of the statements and the map, even if he did not wish to appear foolish, by not questioning the postulations of the psychologist, who may have raised the question as to why he was on the bench, if he could not accept the fabrics so fine, that are what British Justice is based upon, should be obvious to a neurotic Judge or anyone thinking with the clarity of a child.

Including various other statements and the coroner's reports, also it should be noted most of the statements are the first statements made, not those after cross-examination, where the overlooked details were pointed out, but those trial papers are not on hand, i.e. they were written in shorthand, which are destroyed after 5 years, it is also worth noting that on the list of exhibits, No One has signed for any of them, which implies they are still in existence, but the custom it seems use to be, after the trial, all the physical evidence was returned to the police, which must have offered encouragement for the police, to freely pervert the course of justice with immunity.

In fact there is a good possibility some of the physical evidence was destroyed at a later date, when DNA was discovered as a failsafe method of evidence.

Dr Alan Cliff was sacked as the Home Office forensic scientist, not so much for inventing evidence, but for missing out or overlooking vital pieces of information that made no sense to him, he was discredited, after a contemporary report on 17.11.84…a two year review of 1,500 instances in which Dr Cliff examined material was carried out after the High Court in Scotland delivered a broadside against Dr Cliff of almost unprecedented ferocity. About 129 cases where people were convicted after denying the offenses had been checked in detail. Some 16 cases involving 17 men were referred by the Home Secretary to the Appeal Court. Three of these did not want their cases referred, three later abandoned the appeal before its conclusion [probably due to having been released on Mental Health Sections] and two cases were still being traced. Three of the remaining eight had their convictions quashed and five had their appeals dismissed.

None of the responsible bodies concerned with the Dr Cliff affair...the Ombudsman, the Civil Service Appeal Board and the Court of Appeal had questioned the conclusion reached about Dr Cliff!

I will copy out the full statement, made at the indictment hearing, it is also worth noting, that this is the only in the whole case file, that was quoted at the hearing, all the other statements are vague things written within days of the murder.

I feel it is important to copy out Dr Cliff's statement before that of the Police, to enable you to see more clearly some very questionable errors in the police statements, especially when it is taken into consideration that the detective claimed to have unique powers of observation, but failed to see the obvious, because it did not exist initially, but added later, plus with promotion being the obvious conclusion to anyone capable of solving the case immediately with "superior powers" of detection and anyway who would question him, for after all his suspect was a nutter in a mental hospital, who just by luck happened to be from an Approved School charged with attempted GBH, and had already admitted being at the farm, about the time the murder may have been taking place, it stands to reason that with such facts before a court, his conviction was an almost foregone conclusion.

He must have been the happiest "Laughing Policeman" in history when none of his powers of detection were questioned by either Q.C.'s.

A small point to take into consideration, which may seem a bit repetitive to a general reader, but may make sense to a Student of Law, and or future victims of police corruption.

The reply from the Lord Chancellor's Office. 28.4.95.

Indictment Cumberland Summer Assizes held at Carlisle on Monday 15th May 1961.

R.G.Clover Q.C. and Mr G.Halpen [defence]

Evidence of Dr. Allen Cliff.

Sunday 5.3.61 visited Garlands Hospital.

Took exhibits 16, 18, 48, 49 [dust from the scene].

Soil from the store at the farm and a sack from under the church. [Exhibit

No.50] fibres from brick in the barn and hairs from the brick by the slaughterhouse door [Exhibit No.51]. I also collected some string from a cowshed at the farm [Exhibit No.52].

Same day attended P.M. at Mortuary at Cumberland Infirmary and received from Dr Corby Exhibits 6 to 15 inclusive. I took possession of certain clothing from the deceased including Wellingtons produced Exhibit 53, Socks 54, Trousers 55, Underpants, Cardigan, Jersey and Vest 56. Under the Supervision of Dr Corby I took filter paper swabs of the buttocks and tops of legs of the deceased [No.57].

Same day at Carlisle County Police Station, I received from D.C. Burns Exhibits 20, 21 and 23 to 42 inclusive.

7.3.61. I received from the same officer Exhibits43 and 44 and on 8.3.61 Exhibits 5, 17 and 19.

On 15.3.61. I received by registered post Exhibits 22 and 45. I have assessed all these articles.

Blood from Warwick Exhibit 13 and blood Peck Exhibit 20 are of Group A. Blood from scene 43 and 44 is human blood group A and the salvia labelled as coming from Peck Exhibit 45, shows that he is a blood group secretor.

We all have blood groups [born and throughout life] A, B, AB or O. Some people secrete these blood group substances into their body secretions for example saliva, tears, and semen and such people are referred to as secretors. They can do it through nasal secretion. About 30% of people do not secrete blood group substances into their body secretions and these people are referred to as non-secretors. About 40% of people have blood Group A [varies from one part of Great Britain to another and that is approximate for North of England].

Trousers Exhibit 28 has a small human blood group A stain at the bottom front of the left leg. There is a small seminal stain on the inside of the left side of the fly opening. I am not able to say how old the stain was. There were three buttons on the fly of the trousers when I received them. The next to the bottom button was missing. The buttons remaining on the trousers are indistinguishable from the button from the scene Exhibit No.39 which was clean when I received it. The buttons on the trousers appear to have been stitched on by a machine. Because of this method of stitching I was easily able to free a button from the trousers together with its stitching thread by slipping one load of thread over another at the back of the fly and gently pulling the button. The stitching thread was 7.8" in length and is now produced Exhibit 58. The thread from the glans penis, Exhibit No.23, is 7.6" in length, both pieces of are similar in colour and structure.

The top of the shoe Exhibit No.30 is made of a basket work like pattern. In the crevices of which there is a relatively large amount of human Group A blood.

The absence of blood on the upper surface of this pattern indicates that it must have been wiped off. There is human Group A blood inside the left toe and some of this was wet when I examined it on Sunday 5.3.61.

Both shoes Exhibits 30 and 31 have lime, manure, soil, sand and chaff on the soles. The dust from the scene. Exhibit 49 includes lime, manure, soil, sand and chaff. Similar materials was also found on the left turn-up, Exhibit 28.

The sweepings from the office floor, Exhibit 41, include pieces of chaff and sand.

The left sock, Exhibit 33, has human blood Group A on the top of the toe, the underpants, Exhibit 35, have seminal staining on the front.

The string from the pocket, Exhibit 37, consist of 2 pieces, one is similar to agricultural twine and has a typical machine knot in one end. The string differs from that on the hands of Warwick, Exhibit 15. The other piece of string is thin cord.

String from the cowshed, Exhibit 52, is similar to agricultural twine and has in one end a typical machine tied knot similar to the knot in one of the pieces of string of Exhibit 37. I saw many pieces of string like Exhibit 52 at Garlands Hospital farm. It differs in colour from the string on the hands of Warwick, Exhibit 15, but it has several other factors similar to this string Exhibit 15.

Hairs from the blood at the scene, Exhibit 40, are similar to the head hair of Warwick, Exhibit 12, some of these hairs appear to have been cut at both ends. One normally expects the hair of a male person to be cut at one end. The appearance of this hair cut at both ends is consistent with it being cut off with a weapon. I am not able to say whether by a sharp or blunt weapon. If this boy had been hit on the head even by a blunt weapon then the hairs may have been cut.

Instrument perhaps would be a better word than weapon. I was not able to find any instrument at the farm which had human hairs on it. Other than articles in the pool of blood in the pen, I could not find any article which had blood on it.

The material from the middle finger right hand, Exhibit No.25, is a small amount of sand and human blood. On the swab from the top of the left leg, part of Exhibit 57, I found a seminal stain.

The finger nail cuttings of Warwick, Exhibit No, 14, have on one left finger nail a royal blue fibre similar to the fibres of which the jacket of Peck, Exhibit 36, is made.

The dirt from the front of the neck and right buttock, Exhibits 11 to 16 included sand.

The stomach contents Exhibit 13, includes material which appears to be potato and onions.

The string from the hands, Exhibit 15, is tied with a reef knot. The string is similar to agricultural twine and is thicker than the string from the pocket, Exhibit 37.

The trousers, Exhibit 55, have seminal staining on the outside of the right button, on the inside of the right buttock and on the right shoulder strap. Some of this has been tested and has come from a person whose blood is of Group A and who is a secretor.

The Wellingtons, Exhibit 53, have sand on the soles and inside.

The socks, Exhibit 54, have sand on them, most of it being on the toes.

The clothing Exhibits 48 and 56 have sand on them.

The khaki hanky from the scene, Exhibit 18, is marked with ink in one corner, the marking appears to be "30".On the hanky there are many human Group A bloodstains and a hair which is similar to that from Warwick, Exhibit 12 and Peck, Exhibit 26.

The hanky is similar to the control khaki hanky, Exhibit 19, I have not been able to find any significant differences between them.

The white hanky from the scene, Exhibit 16, is marked with a figure "42" in ink in one corner. The hanky has many Group A human blood stains on it and is similar to the control white hanky Exhibit 17. I have not been able to find any significant difference between Exhibits 16 and 17. There is a nasal secretion on the hankies, Exhibits 16 and 18 and test on these indicate that it has come from a person who has blood Group A and is a secretor.

The sock, Exhibit 22, is stained with blood, but this blood is not of human origin.

The brick, Exhibit 5 does not have any human hairs on it. There is blood on it.

There was nothing significant on Exhibits 7 to 10 inclusive from Peck, 27 the urine, 42 nail clippings, 50 the socks and 51 the fibre and hairs from bricks at the scene.

Here are some points worth noting before reading the statement of D/Sgt. No 24. Albert Launder.

On 15.3.61. Dr Cliff receives by post, [ten days after the murder] the sock Exhibit 22, that is stained with non-human blood.

The seminal stain found on my trousers, Dr.Cliff was unable to say how old the stain was…having received them less than 18 hours after the murder had taken place [according to the estimated time of death] so there must have been some difference, between a recent smear and an old one.

The thread from my button being found in my glans penis, obviously didn't just fall out, having had to pass into my underpants, as Dr Cliff states; he had to pull gently on the button, after releasing the thread to get it out in one piece, whereas anyone who has lost a button off an article of clothing, will appreciate, it takes some time for the thread to come out, because the knot is inside of the cloth, not released by hand, but usually broken from the outside.

Also the button was found to be clean when handed to Dr Cliff, even though in the photographs, it was found on top of a bag of cement dust and the ground was wet, plus in one of the police statements I had told them I lost it a week or so earlier and it had fallen into a drainage channel, but then how long does it take to rub cement powder off a button or clean a button and drop it into a bag of cement? Also has anyone noticed that cement doesn't remain as powder dust after it has been rained on?

Note the top of the shoe was a basket work pattern and the blood was only found in the crevices, yet none was found on the surface of the shoe or under the basket work pattern or on the sock, also he mentions finding blood inside the toe of the shoe and some of it was still wet when he examined it the next day, also there was human blood on top of the toe of the sock Exhibit 33. Yet no blood was found anywhere else on the shoe or on the sock.

I will cover the above point in more detail after the police statement, which points out that before the police took my shoes away from me, there had been some bloody matter on them from the compost heap, maybe it was an extremely hot March evening and the blood had dried and fallen off, when the shoes bent slightly when climbing up the stairs.

Maybe March 1961 was the hottest month since the evolution of the earth and Cumberland was inundated with volcano's and earthquakes, so as the world was about to end, then why not frame the first candidate to come along, no one will be left alive to disprove such a heat wave or a crime against an innocent person and anyway if anyone should survive, this evidence will be kept secret by the Home Office and nobody, least of all the accursed or accused, will ever have access to it.

The string the boy was tied up with, was completely different in thickness and colour, to that found in my pockets…later you will discover why I had told the police about the string.

The reference to the sack from the church, may be because I had pointed out in the statement, that I had gone to the back of the church, to fill some holes, where I had dug up some flowers for my visitor, but as far as I can make out, the sack was a figment of the police's imagination, even though one was found later in some machinery, but by a strange coincident, this too was covered only in animal blood.

Okay a lot of things did not appear at the beginning of the book, such as the flowers I had dug up, it was a long time ago and I had only remembered more important things, reading these statements brought back a lot of memories.

The seminal stains were not given any test, other than they were from Group

A secretor, which was the same as 40% of the people in that area, which I was not only having lived up north for 4 months, so had he jumped to a wrong conclusion, as to where I was from.

They were not even tested to see if they were my own, because there were a lot of strange guys in the hospital, who a kid would not say No to, if being interfered with, after what had taken place in the Approved School or in the lodgings, that resulted in GBH and being sent North, the chances are if any test had been carried out, it would have emerged there were several different groups present in or on my trousers.

As to my blood group being an A…okay, but not your communal A or AB… in fact my group covers maybe only 5% of the population [maybe the world population, considering the numbers of international request for such donors, but each time I have made contact, it proved pointless as my group is the same, hence if I were to give blood at 9 a.m. and needed some at 5 p.m., I cannot have my donated blood back] because my blood group is; " Rh: A.ccdd'E, positive donor, negative recipient!", not uncommon, but definitely not your garden variety of Group A… but as pointed out, already Dr Cliff had a habit of ignoring what he did to know… which in some ways is better than inventing evidence…but only just better.

On one of the hankies was a hair similar to both mine and the boy, yet the boy had completely different coloured hair from my own.

The observation of the hankies was sadly not observed as being in biro and not Indian ink as the school used, I can recall quite vividly the school's matron arguing in the court on the point and no one ever argues with the matron.

Accept the observation that there was no difference between the materials of the hankies, found at the scene, with those in the school and were on general sale throughout the country, as two cotton hankies, the only difference he observed were the numbers, but not that they were in different ink types.

There were also several references to main barn, well apart from pointing out I had played there earlier in the day, it seems a lot of things were looked for in the barn, it makes even more interesting reading, when it appears that a Detective Sargent with very acute powers of observation, cannot tell the difference between a Dutch Barn and general Farm Buildings.

I think that is just enough to be going on with.

Before going on to the first of the police statements, I will cover statements [that I have] of the witness's and some general observations taken from statements, because I did not have enough time to copy out everything word for word, but anyone who can access these statements, will also note that I have not deliberately erased any important details, in fact they will read as unbiased, because some on the surface appear to be incriminating, but then why else should they remain in existence?

Yet the police statements were photocopied so they are completely faithful in their reproduction.

1. Colin Corby, Lecturer in Forensic Medicine, University of Durham and Pathologist to the Royal Victoria Infirmary, Newcastle and to the Home Office North Forensic Laboratory.

   Post Mortem Findings: Anus. Soiled faces and appears a little dilated admitting a finger quite easily, but could find no recent tears or old scarring. Normal but slightly lax. Condition was not consistent with a male penis having been there.

   Cause of death, Brain Haemorrhage and a fractured skull.

2. Dr W C Menzies. Reg. Medical Practitioner. Examined Peck 4.3.61. At 11.15 p.m. No bloodstains on body. No injury to penis or signs of sexual matter.

   On penis I found a thread of dark material Exhibit 23. At the end of the penis partly under the foreskin. Took swab from penis, Exhibit 24. Scrapings from under finger nail of right middle finger, Exhibit 25. Pubic hair and scalp hair, Exhibit 26. Hand over to Police Officer, D/Sgt Launder.

   *Note the lack of signs indicating recent sex, either intercourse or masturbation, not even on the thread, it is also worth noting that having a foreskin, any residue of recent or previous day ejaculations, would have been trapped in the foreskin, but the swab proved negative, I had not recently had a bath or washed that part of my body, then the thread would not have been there either.

3. John Paton: A male nurse was in the farm yard with his daughter at about 1.15.saw Peck and the children just outside the farmyard. He asked Peck if they were his gang, but Peck did not reply, at 1.30 saw Peck again outside the front door of the hospital.

4. Marjorie Warwick [no relation to the deceased] stated that Peck delivered a package to her ward at about 3.50 p.m.

   *Note the time she claims was 3.50 p.m. although the bus my visitor left on did not leave until 4 p.m.

5. William Johnson saw Peck between 3.50 to 4.00 p.m. just outside the farm yard from approximately 40 yards away, and 20 yards from the farm gate, walking slowly across the grass, then approached 3 little girls on the sand heap…he was not in the farm between 4.10 and 4.50 p.m.

* Isn't that strange, I was then seen again at 3.50p.m. quite some distance away in the opposite direction, regardless of the fact I was seen heading to the farm by a witness, who pointed out I had been on my own.

6. Philomena Murphy, states she was with Virginia Story and her sister, when she saw Peck the second time, the first being near the canteen with George Warwick, then the second time he spoke to them in the sand, no one else was with him. After talking to them for a while he left them and walked towards the farm, then she went back to where the boys were playing, but George was not with them.

*Now its four witnesses, to confirm that I went to the farm alone, also later in the police statement, I had met the girls earlier, with my visitor who had a kitten on a lead, which was why I stopped the second time to talk with them, when they asked where the kitten was.

Also if she had seen me behind the canteen with George, before I left him at the end of the short path and headed across the road to the church, to fill in some holes I had made earlier, then saw me heading towards the farm on my own, this raises two questions, were the police getting witnesses to say; I was in two different places at 3.50 p.m. regardless of the fact I had strong confirmation, I had definitely been somewhere else, before going to the female ward at approximately 4.05p.m.

It would appear it was necessary for me to be somewhere else 25 minutes earlier, to be able to commit the murder, then retraced all my footsteps, hoping I would have witnesses to say; I was heading to the farm alone, but the snag was; It was confirmed, I had been seen by several witnesses, at a bus stop at 4.p.m. who for some obscure reason, were never asked to give evidence or their statements became "misplaced"!

7. Search for the boy started about 8.20 p.m. says Joe Briggs. He found the body between 9.10 and 9.15 p.m. and took the body to the gardeners shop.

8. Arthur Haugh stated I went with him into the slaughter house for a look around and chatted with him, and then states he did not hear the button fall off or see it on the ground and I left with him. He also claimed the hankies were in the bucket two days earlier.

*Two small points, he states he did not hear the button fall; also I would not have relieved myself inside the building when there was a large yard outside. The point about the hankies, the police claim they found them in a different building, then asking it they were mine, I denied they were, after taking them to where I said they would be, now ask yourselves, if I had claimed they were not my hankies, then why did the police need to find a witness to suggest they had been there a week earlier?

He then claimed the visit to the slaughter house, had taken place a week earlier, although this interview took place sometime after the murder, so did he imply: it took place a week before the murder or a week before his interview? Because for it to take place a week earlier meant the combined harvester arrived the previous Saturday, before I had my visitor, so why mention it.

9. Robert Lee [nurse] said he took a blood sample on 15th February, when the syringe broke causing blood to run over my wrist and onto my trousers, a student nurse swabbed it with cotton wool.

10. Thomas Ellwood said he was on duty during the afternoon of 4th March and noticed me sitting in front of the TV at between 4.45 and 4.50, but he added he had not seen me earlier, as he was serving out the medication.

11. Richard Hall aged 7, said I approached them in their den, and two of his friends followed me towards the church, but only one came back, that was the last time he saw George.

     *It should be pointed out here, that Richard pointed out we had walked towards the "church" which was at the end of the path, but later suggested; he saw me walking in the direction of the farm, which would have been an impossibility.

12. Football results came on at 4.41.p.m.

Yet there were no statements made by myself, except a dubious one by the police, just before being arrested, that is unsigned by anyone, there was not even a statement from Miss Dawson, my main witness, who I had spent the afternoon with, plus there was not a statement, made by a mysterious witness, who turned up in court 9-10 weeks after the murder, who said he saw me walking from the church, hand in hand with the boy towards the farm, now although he managed to describe what both of us were wearing, he failed to see the 3 girls or the other farm labourer, who vouched for the fact I had been on my own.

It is also worth noting, he saw me walking towards the farm from the direction of the church, where I had been filling in some holes, but why did it take a farm labourer so long to offer evidence that should have been in the deposition at the first court hearing. Why wait so long, he must have seen the police around the farm for at least a week after the murder and stranger still, not only did he claim he saw me and the boy heading towards the farm, but described us in perfect detail.

Okay I only had the one set of clothing and everyone at the hospital, could have described me in perfect detail, but how many people could have described what the child had been wearing in detail, plus what he failed to observe, was that from the church to the farm, I was also seen by four other witnesses, three who knew the boy very well, but they had pointed out I was alone, which was also witnessed by William Johnson.

Later it will be observed, that the only place this witness, could have seen me walking from the church to the farm, without seeing the four witnesses, would have been where the murder had taken place.

I will put the first police statement in a separate chapter, as this one is getting a bit long.

* * * * *

Chapter 2
D/Sgt Launder's Statement

This is an exact copy of D/Sgt Launders statement and I will add numbers in brackets for later comments…

This witness Albert Launder on oath says:

At 8.25 p.m. On Saturday 4th March 1961, I arrived at Garlands Hospital, Carlisle. Some five minutes later I saw the Accursed Malcolm Peck in a room in the hospital with P.C. Watson. With D/C. Burns I questioned the Accused Peck. I asked him where he had left the child meaning the deceased and he said [1] he left him at the corner of the laundry at about 4.30 p.m. and [2] prior to that he had been playing in the bushes near the canteen with eight other children.

I made a search of the bushes but could not find the child. At 8.45 p.m. Supt. Milne and Supt Oldcorn asked the accused where he had left the child and the accused gave a similar explanation to that which he had previously given me and went on and described what the deceased whom he called [3] "kiddah" was wearing. He said he was wearing maroon pants, a yellow pullover, was the only one wearing yellow, he didn't know the child's name, but said [4] that three had rifles, [5] a ginger boy had a stick 18" long by 1" wide, had boots on, one was wearing black jeans, one was carrying a toy Winchester, one had a space rifle and one had two holsters. He said left six children in the bushes and when he left there two of the children followed him, one left him behind the Occupational Therapy building [which he described as "O.T"], the other [6] child "Kiddah" came to the corner of the laundry. As the result of a message I left Peck. I went to a place on the east side of the hospital workshops. There I saw witness Joseph Briggs who pointed out to me the body of the deceased which was in the position shown in photograph 1 of Exhibit No.3.

With other officers I went with Mr. Briggs to the pens on the north side of the slaughterhouse in the farm yard. He pointed out a spot there to me which is the place shown in photograph 2 of Exhibit No.3. In the western corner of the pen into which the slaughterhouse doors open I saw a [7] large pool of blood approximately 4ft long and some 2ft from the lower dividing wall.

Between the pool of blood and the dividing wall there was [8] a clean button. This button is Exhibit No.39. It was in the position shown in photographs 5 and 6 of Exhibit No.3.

A pair of child's mittens were lying on the lower dividing wall [9]. They are produced Exhibit No.48. There were two pieces of cloth both heavily blood stained one khaki and one white, lying at the north side of the pen. [9] They are Exhibits No's 16 and 18. They were in the position shown in photograph 2 and 3 of Exhibit No.3.

Arrangements were made for the scene to be guarded by Sgt. Morton and at 9.50 p.m. with D/Supt. Oldcorn I again saw the accused, I told him that the child's body had been found and then took pocession of his shoes. As I was doing so Peck said "I know they have straw on because I was over at the farm this morning." [11] I then pointed out the wet matter on the left shoe and asked what it was. He said "It's some stuff off the compost heap". "I was looking for eggs, I got one once." I asked him if he had a handkerchief and he said "I haven't got nothing, I washed it the other day and it disappeared" I then asked if he had any other clothing and he said "This is junk anyway, it's from the school. I haven't got any more."

He was then asked where he left the boy and he said across from the [12] laundry about 4.30 p.m. I pointed out what appeared to be blood stains on his trousers and he said "They are not. They have been like that since I came here." I asked him if he had been bleeding at any time and he said [13] "Yes when they took some blood from me a bit ago. It broke and the blood went on my pants" He was then asked where the child had gone when he left him and he said "He was going back to his mates."

Arrangements were made for the Accused to be medically examined by Dr. Menzies. [14] Prior to that examination D/Con. Burns took possession of the Accused's shoes and clothing. After the Accused had been stripped of his clothing [15] I noticed a piece of thread on his penis. When Dr. Menzies commenced his examination I pointed out the thread to him and Dr. Menzies removed it. I then took possession of the thread Exhibit No. 23 and exhibits Nos. 24, 25 and 26, I handed them to D/Con. Burns at 11.30 p.m.

[16] I saw a small scratch mark on the back of the Accused's forefinger, two marks on the back of his neck which may have been old boil scars and a scab on the front of his left foot. They were not recent.

Following the medical examination with Supt. Oldcorn I again saw Peck. I questioned him about his movements throughout the day. He said he got up at 7 a.m. put mattress on his bed, went to the toilet, made his bed got dressed and went downstairs. After describing what had happened in the morning he told me what happened about 1.30 p.m.

[17] He said that at 1.30 p.m. he saw the bus coming up to the hospital and he went to meet Miss Dawson. He stayed with her until 4 o'clock. He said she had a cat with her. He said they talked for a while and played with the cat, she had some food with her and after she left delivered a parcel from her to the female ward. He said she had a cat on a lead and they went for a walk around the grounds and three or four boys came up to him and he gave [18] one of the boys some biscuits.

He said the little boy with [19] ginger hair asked him for a stick about 4.15 p.m. and said they would come back at 9 a.m. except one who was a catholic and he would be there at 10.30 a.m. the following morning. He told the boys about bows and arrows and walked away, one went back [20] across the road from the church and the other boy was told to go but followed him. [21] That was the ginger boy. He told him he would have to go for his tea and left the boy at the corner of the laundry and went into the hospital. He then went straight into the toilets, rinsed his hands, dried them on his trousers because his hands weren't very wet. He then went into Ward B, typewriter with football results on TV. He then sat and watched the following programs on t.v. When he left the boy he said that two men in an ambulance went pass and he told the boy to stand against the wall. He also said that a German from Ward 9 saw him with the boy, [22] and he wiped his shoes on a sack that morning saying the sack was in the barn, there was meat and that on them off the compost heap. He said "I got an egg off there once."

When told that the matter on his shoe looked like blood he said "It looks like blood it will be cow, pig or chicken." [23] Asked if it was there when Miss Dawson came he said it was. Asked if he had been in the barn he said "Yes I walked through it about half past twelve or a quarter to one." At 2.30 a.m. he accompanied us to the barn where we made a search for the sack. The barn is among the farm buildings marked [24] R on the plan Exhibit No.1. We were unable to find the sack. Whilst we were in I saw [25] a bucket containing what looked blood stained water and a blood stained handkerchief. The Handkerchief is Exhibit No.21. I asked him if it were his [26] and he denied it was saying "I would know mine. It had a big hole in it near the corner." He then examined the handkerchief and said it was not his.

At 3 a.m. we returned to the hospital and he remembered that at 12.30 p.m. the previous day 4th March, he had taken two pieces of stew meat to the dog in the farm yard at about 12.30 p.m. [27] and had never been back to the farm after that.

At 9.30 a.m. on 5th March I was present at the mortuary at the Cumberland Infirmary when Dr. Corby carried out a post mortem examination upon the body of the deceased boy. [28] At that time it was noticed that the boy's hands were tied behind his back with course binder twine.

[29] The boy's hair was blond or fair. After the post mortem examination I went with Dr. Corby to the pen behind the slaughterhouse and pointed out the pen to him. After the post mortem examination I was present when Dr. Cliff made his examination of the scene and surrounds. I pointed out various places to him. [30] I again made a search of the barn to which I have already referred to but was not able to find any sack. I then examined the dung heap marked with a "U" on the plan Exhibit No.1. The heap measured approximately 5ft high by 4yds broad by 7yds long. It was composed mostly of straw and found the surface sufficiently firm to walk on. There was no blood apparent on top of the heap but on the south east corner there [33] were some entrails which were only partially covered by straw and fairly dry. The surface of the heap itself was relatively dry.

At about 3.p.m. on 6th March 1961, with D/Supt. Oldcorn I saw the Accused in the presence of his solicitor. The Accused was questioned and he replied to questions. Notes of the interview were taken by Miss Ellwood. The interview was concluded at 4.5 p.m. At 6.30 p.m. I arrested the Accused at Garlands Hospital and took him to the County Police Station at Carlisle. At 7p.m. I cautioned and charged the Accused with murdering George Taylor Warwick and he replied "I didn't ".

On 7th March 1961 I took possession of the brick Exhibit No.5. It was in the pen where the child's body was found. I later handed it to D/Con. Burns and on 14th March 1961 with Supt. Oldcorn I examined the slaughterhouse and drains. In the centre section of the slaughterhouse there are two floor channels which take the water into a tile through the slaughterhouse wall and then into an outside drain. The grill of the west channel is a fixture and the drain empties into a manhole cover in the next pen to where the child's body was found. This underground drain travels for a distance of 7 to 8ft before entering the manhole cover, and in that distance falls approximately 4 feet.

In order to test the efficiency of the drain I inserted a hose pipe into the tile in the slaughterhouse wall and with the tap full on found the drain to be more than adequate to accommodate the flush of water, there was no back wash into the pen.

[32] We placed a trouser button into the centre of the slaughterhouse door opening and using the hose pipe washed it out into the pen where the child's body

was found. The water and the button drained into a water channel on the extreme northern side of the pen, and no water washed into the western side of the pen. [33] The vision from the sand heap to the dipping pens is good and is about 50 yards.

Signed by Albert Launder and witnessed by T.H.Rothidge or Rotlidge.

*   *   *   *   *

I am going to make a lot of comments here, because one small error or even half a dozen slight errors can be forgiven, but 33 errors that were never queried in the court, sound just a little bit too farfetched to be true.

But the really clever bit, took over a year to figure it out…

Note all the way through his statement I had repeatedly made reference to the little ginger haired kid and I was conned into thinking, he was the child that had died, but he got a bit too clever by inserting what the murdered child had been wearing, then claiming I had described his clothing, without even seeing him for more than a glance maybe…I hadn't met him [unless it was the child who followed me, but it was so briefly I didn't take much notice, whereas the boy I had been with and his two friends, I had picked up several times to look into pens etcetera…don't forget when I was at the farm with them, at exactly the same time as the farmer saw his son, with someone wearing the clothing of a hospital near the powerhouse.

Well read as written, You can appreciate that; to someone going through the files looking for errors, that may prove the Home Office is obviously aware of the Truth and covering Itself, i.e. like no statements of My Main Witness and My Own Signed Statement, the above police statement could look; simple and straightforward, but then they were confident, that anyone who could discredit it, would never gain access to the files.

I read it several times over the week and kept saying; "This is a load of crap!" But how can I prove it, and then did something; it was obvious the Home Office overlooked doing; I compared his statement with the Map of the Hospital Exhibit No.1. Because I have remembered all my life taking them to the farm office, to show them where I had placed the hanky in the bucket, I have no idea where the sack came into it.

He stated No.24. That I had taken him to the barn marked "R" on the plan and later said; No.30. He returned to the barn to which he had already referred, but was unable to discover the sack.

Now it just so happens that the place , he referred to as taking me to, to look for the sack, was in fact exactly where I had taken them to find my hankies…the barn is clearly marked on the Plan as; "Building Q!"

Not a very observant Policeman!

That was said in jest, but not on that one small point, as he seems to have given me greater powers of observation than he had himself, whilst at the same time making me sound like a demented psychologically disturbed idiot, in a mental hospital, which would run around the farm at every conceivable moment to find an egg, okay I admit I use to go over there searching for eggs each evening, but read the statement again...

Nos.1, 6 and 12. It states I left the child at the laundry at 4.30 p.m. which was just across the square from my ward, but it also said several times I had been playing with the children at 4.15 p.m. a distance of 500 yards from the laundry, but hardly a 15 minute walk, although it may be added that the laundry was almost in an unobstructed line, from where the girls were playing.

To reach the laundry from where the children were playing meant walking along a road with no footpath, with a lot of traffic on it, buses, ambulances, visitor's cars and various patients, which proves in a small way, I was being made to look like I was lying. It was also the road to the farm, but at the laundry it opened onto the square, with a roundabout in the middle, where patients, staff and visitors would have seen me and the child, had we been together.

Think about it this way, if I were seeking an alibi, I would hardly say; I had left him at the laundry, where I would have had dozens of witnesses, had I been with the child at the square, another small point worthy of note, is that except No.1. the first time, when the time was 4.30 p.m. is followed by having to leave the interview, as He goes on to talk about unrelated things, note this was more or less a general conversation, not a statement being made by me, whilst helping the police with their enquiries, he wasn't taking notes, so why did he remember, the last thing I had said, when his mind was distracted the moment I said it.

It seems obvious he needed to imply; I had said it 3 times, to prove I must be guilty by lying, because other people could have seen me with the child, but nobody did, because the child wasn't with me.

Yet if we return to the statement of Philomena Murphy, who I had pointed out to the police as an alibi, that I had walked from behind the church, towards the farm and that I had been alone, it is also worth noting, that nowhere in his statement were those children mentioned, plus their statements of events, were also confirmed by William Johnson who was working in the farm yard, even though he was persuaded by the police to imply; I had been with the girls 25 minutes earlier, than was physically possible, as my visitor did not leave until 4 p.m..

Also it would appear he must have thought; I was a zombie on medication, who would not have enough sense to run away after murdering a child, but calmly walk back to my ward and sit watching the TV. as if nothing had happened, anyone that callous and unmoved, would not deny it, but just drone off all the details, in an uninterested matter of fact way.

The same as most of the child killers, in Broadmoor had done and may well be discussing in every detail.

Think about the information we already have about and implied about me, I was from an approved school, where I had smashed the dormitory window for no reason whatsoever , I was also in there for attempted GBH, so that makes me an extremely violent anarchist .

I was also in my second mental hospital for observation, therefore obviously a few screws loose, later it was discovered I had a thread in my foreskin, implying I rarely washed myself or was incapable of doing so unsupervised, I spent all day at the farm looking for eggs, plus I was also lacking in any form of human emotions.

Now a person completely lacking in emotions, especially a mental patient, could not be anything other than a psychopath or schizophrenic, yet they were not aware at that time, when I was a suitable candidate for a perfect frame up, that I was not on any medication or undergoing treatment, I also had to bathe most mornings, because of my incontinence and I had worked on a dairy and poultry farm, so had some idea, when to look for eggs.

Yet again I digress.

2. prior to leaving the child at the laundry a 4.30.p.m. I had been playing with about eight children in the bushes near the canteen.

I had gone to see the kids at about 4.15.p.m. to make arrangements for the next day, but the way it reads, it seems to imply; I claimed I was playing with them for just over half an hour…from 3.50 p.m. to 4.25.? as it was only a few minutes' walk to the laundry, if the bushes are still there, it will be observed they were ever-greens in a landscaped area, not an overgrown thicket.

Now I have never denied; I went to see the children to make arrangements for the next day or that two followed me, thinking I was going to make the bows immediately, but I was only with them from arriving to leaving the youngest child at the end of the path, all in all a few minutes.

Now look at No.19. Quote; "He said the little boy with ginger hair, asked for a stick at about 4.15 p.m." it would seem I was doing a lot of things in various places at 4.15.p.m.

Why should the little boy ask me for a stick, when it had already been explained earlier by this observant policeman, who don't forget was not taking any written notes, as this is all part of a general conversations whilst helping with their enquiries, because if we return to No's. 3-5 inclusive, it will be noted that; not only was I capable of describing what each child had been wearing, but also what they had been carrying, a pretty amazing feat of memory for a few minutes of conversation and thinking they were the same kids, I had played with at the farm, at 12.30. p.m. but then there were three of them, that rapidly increased to eight kids in the bushes, that I had played with All the afternoon, including the farmer's son, who according to the father wasn't even at the farm, when I was with the three kids!

Yet to return to No.19…why should a kid ask for a stick at 4.15 p.m.? When in No.5. Quote: "A ginger haired boy had a stick 18" long by 1" wide."

There "was" only, One Child with Ginger Hair!

It goes on to mention the laundry again, which on the plan is marked "L" whereas, where I had left the child, was near "H" the canteen at the end of the path.

I add this because; Although until I went to the Lord Chancellors Office, I had no idea about the hospital plans or the symbols of each building, unlike the police who did have reference plans, being a patient free to wander around, I would have been fully aware of what the buildings were called, so would not have mistaken the canteen, for the laundry however psychologically deficient, they made me appear or took for granted when deciding how easy it would be to frame me.

Although one should query why he never read his own statement after writing it or could it be; he was confident that no one would question the word of a Detective [Defective] Sargent, made on oath or derogative oaths?

In No's. 5. 19 and 21 I made repeated references to; "The Ginger Boy"

In No.18 I point out I had given one of the boys biscuits, this was the Ginger haired boy, it is very probable that the child did not follow me for a bow, but in the hope of some more biscuits, also it is very probable he had no idea, I was returning the next day to make bows.

I will explain why I put this in, The Boy I had been describing to the police, thinking he was the one that was missing, with extremely fresh memories of the ginger haired child, who had been with some other boys earlier in the day and who I had given biscuits to in the afternoon.

When I was in court, I distinctly remember the post mortem results, not making any reference to biscuits in the child's stomach contents, just potatoes and onions, whereas biscuits eaten a few hours later would not have digested before the previous food intake.

Also if you go back to No.29. It is observed that; "The boy's hair was blonde or fair!"

Now it is almost impossible to mistake Ginger as anything other than Ginger, add to this the biscuits and the question that comes to mind, is just who was the child I had been describing and how did I get charged with murdering a child I had not knowingly met, but the police had allowed me to think it was the same child, as followed me to the end of the path, note I hadn't been taking much notice, otherwise I would have sent him back with the other boy who had followed me.

The oddest part is; that the other children said it was George who had followed me, but then I thought I was alone, the chances are I did not take much notice of the child's appearance [it's like going into a shop with three customers in it, and then as you leave are expected to describe every one of them, especially if they are all strangers to you]when I told him I would be back the next day, yet I have always remembered the child had ginger hair, it was only when I read these statements, did I discover the child had blonde hair, but I do remember that the child I had been referring to, was the child I had given biscuits to, it was the stomach contents, that have always caused another question mark to be branded in my mind.

If we return to No.4. It seems I had been very precise in what each boy had been carrying, yet I apparently mistaken the colour of the boy's hair, which is something I had not seen at a glance, but then considering I had only been with the boy's in the bushes a few minutes, it's hardly possible I could have known what each child was carrying and less likely D/Sgt Launder would have remembered such fine details, especially as soon as I apparently given him given him the details, he was called away and taken to the place where the child's body was.

Okay I know I am a bit cynical sometimes, but I cannot imagine anyone memorising such fine details of guns, sticks and clothing, when confronted by the body of a murdered child, then remain unmoved, as he makes mental notes of otherwise insignificant details, that will be faithfully recorded at some later date , let alone stitching up an obviously innocent person, knowing full well there is a baby killer still at large…just to have a feather in his hat or could it be a case of promotion and a really healthy pension for his rank when he retires.

Now to cover more of D/Sgt Launders Power of Acute Observation, having already covered his Perfect Memory capabilities.

No.11. After telling me the child's body had been found, he took my shoes away from me, quote; "I know they have straw on them, because I was over at the farm this morning…" then he said; "I pointed out some wet matter on the left shoe and asked what it was." He said it was some stuff off the compost heap.

Yet when the shoes were examined by Dr. Clift and Dr. Corby, there wasn't any blood or stuff on the outer surfaces of the shoes, just in the basket weave pattern and inside the toe of the shoe, note nowhere else on the shoe or sock was any blood or blood stains found…?

What happened to the blood and straw?

Did it rapidly dry and disintegrate inside a plastic bag?

But I digress; let's return to observing how great were the powers of observation of this Highly Trained Detective, He noticed I had dried blood stains on my trousers [13], which was my own blood group, confirmed by Dr. Clift and Nurse Lee who had taken a blood sample, when the needle broke, so why did he need to include them in his statement, after discovering from two medical people, they were old and of no consequence to his investigation.

Note before Dr. Menzies medically examines me… [No.14.] two policemen had made me get undressed and took possession of my clothing.

Now this should be obvious to everyone, as well as any policemen reading this; it was a figment of His imagination, i.e. what he is claiming is; That with D/Con Burns he took a 16 year old somewhere and stripped him, then marched him naked to be examined by a doctor, after taking in as many physical details as possible, such as the thread in my foreskin…this statement seems to imply a new slant on "Bent Coppers" who had a side line of picking up young boys and on any pretence having them strip off, without a doctor or medical officer present.

Although where the medical examination took place, there were a lot of people, it was the control point for the search for the child, and also where I flippantly joked about Southend "Always" winning at football.

During the medical examination, he lets us know again how observant he is; [No.16] quote; I saw a small scratch mark on the back of the Accused's left forefinger, two marks on the back of his neck which may have been old boil scars and a scab on his left foot."

When did this "small scratch mark" appear on my finger, before or after blood and sand was found in the child's finger nail, note a small scratch, unlike a cut, rarely draws much blood, but if it had wouldn't the doctor taking my finger nail clipping, have notice it being a lot closer to me than that eagle eyed detective, stood on the other side of the room or did the doctor have a guide-dog with him.

Also in No.9. The child's mittens were found on the small wall, if the child had been wearing mittens before he was killed, how did he get blood and sand in his finger nails, let alone a fibre from my jacket, that was in the care of D/Con Launders until the next morning, it is also worth noting, that when I apparently described what each child had been wearing and carrying, I made no reference to mittens, which on a bright sunny day, would have been very obvious.

Was he just blowing his own trumpet of being so observant or had he created an entire orchestra to impress a jury of tone deaf musicians, who were convinced never to question those in authority.

He had already pointed out the thread in my foreskin to the Doctor, who I am sure wasn't so short sighted, he failed to notice it, when taking swabs for signs of sexual matter.

The results of which proved negative, plus I hadn't recently had a bath or a wash in that area of my body.

Although in the statement it was pointed out, that when I returned to the ward I had washed my hands and wiped them on my trousers.

Now let's return to the observations of the scars etc., he observed during the examination and it goes without saying, that when I took my clothing off, it was in the presence of the doctor and everyone else in the room.

I am not sure if I stripped from the waist up or down, but one thing everyone knows; [including women wearing slacks or jeans] and will appreciate is to remove my trousers, it requires taking my shoes off first, which meant that when I handed them over, I was stood in my socks, which were moved one at a time, when having my toe nails clipped.

Now it has been stated by Dr. Clift and Dr. Corby that the next morning at the post mortem, they found inside the toe shoe of the shoe and on the toe of my sock; "wet blood", but No One, Not Even the Sharp Eyed Detective, nor the Doctor or Anyone else present, saw wet blood on the toe of my sock. Nor was there any blood on my big toe or in the toe nail, the night before!

Think about it this way: The next day wet blood was found inside the toe of the shoe and only on the toe of the sock…weren't the experts curious to know how it got there, without it being on any other part of the shoe or sock, plus the straw wasn't on the shoe either, which should at least raised the question on how it got there, plus it was still wet, implying there must have been a lot of wet blood inside the shoe or did they think I was some weird sort of Freemason ritual, whereby after murdering anyone, the person removes one shoe, then dips their big toe into the blood and very carefully replaces the shoe, without touching the inside of the shoe, so it stays wet indefinitely just on the toe!

The point I am making is: If it had only been a small amount, it would have been obvious, regardless to everyone in the room and had it been water, then over several hours it will have dried up. Plus it was described as a large quantity of blood, so even if I had crossed my feet over each other, there would have been blood on the floor, but let's go back to DR. Clift and Dr. Corby's joint examination, there wasn't any Blood or Straw found on the outside of the shoe, not even in the crevices, just some blood in the basket work pattern, which looked as if it had been wiped off or should we read that as wiped on, because there wasn't any blood anywhere else!

Also yet again we are told in Dr. Clift's statement, that the next morning, that Launder handed him of all the items clothing that had been put in the safe keeping of Launder!

Is it any wonder that the Home Office has placed "A 75 Year Ban on Public Access to these files?!"

Maybe I should put that at the end of this section, but it may help you open your eyes a bit wider, as I point out more observations from this statement, that were not obvious to the Home Office, who allowed this statement to remain in existence, but having said that, they obviously thought I would not find any of these files during my life time to discredit them, but then if they had "tried" to explain my conditions for discharge, maybe my life may have been better [apart from my incontinence], but then if I had never been set up, I would have probably remained almost illiterate and very naïve.

But I digress…

Although it would seem that; these observations have not been put down in any order of importance as I go along, but think about it this way, I am covering points as they appear in the statement, the fact there are a lot of trivial points, is because after each small act of deceit, it becomes obvious he is convincing us, the next major point is just as "True! /?"

The statement is 5 pages long and typed out by someone who is unfamiliar with a type writer, which implies it took him several hours] to type it, several tea breaks and typed over several days.

Let's go on to No's; 22 and 27 incorporating No.11.

In reality I had explained how I got some meat and straw on my shoes, whilst searching for eggs, and had wiped the stuff off with my hanky and placed it in a bucket and filled it with water to soak it over night, they then asked me to take them to the building which is "R" on the plan, to show it to them. Then for reasons known only to himself the hanky became a sack, it changed from evening to midday I got the stuff on my shoes and had walked around all the afternoon with a visitor, with bloody dirty on…which may "only" to be expected from a nutter.

Let me explain it this way, she was a very special person, she had befriended me when I was a long way from home, almost the length of the country, she gave gifts of fruit or sweets and I looked forward to seeing her, she was one of very few people I trusted without question, and she felt good to be with, had I understood the positive emotions of love at that time in my life, I would have been very much In Love with her.

So you should realize, I always looked my best for her visits, trousers pressed under the mattress, clean face and hands and clean shoes! Don't forget I had spent almost my whole life in institutions, where such things were second nature, maybe not to the average adult, so it was pure fantasy to imply I had gone around the whole afternoon, wearing dirty shoes and I wanted her to come whenever possible, so looking like a tramp wouldn't have helped.

Just prior to No.22. it is suggested; I said that a German artist had seen me with the boy, now think about it, had I said he had seen me with the boy, he would have been the perfect witness for the prosecution, in fact the only witness to vouch for the fact I had been at the laundry with the boy, yet he was never called as a witness, because he had seen me on my own, as I walked across the road on my own towards the church.

Then this odd statement follows pointing out the German and for no apparently no reason, I added I had wiped my shoes on a sack that morning, saying the sack was in the barn as I yet again I mention I got an egg there once, as if it were the greatest experience in my life and needed to tell everyone about it, instead of having it explained I went to the farm most evenings to look at the animals and look for eggs, which I found every time and would share with the ward's cook.

In No.23.Asked if it was there before Miss Dawson came, he said it was, wait a moment, he claims to have established that I got meat on my shoes in the morning, so why ask if it was there during the visit, if it was there in the morning and obviously still at night, it must have been on them during the visit, which all these statements imply never took place, even though I had pointed out I had a witness, to prove the fact they had seen me going towards the farm.

At the time of the police asking for help with their enquiries, I didn't know the child had been killed at the farm, so why deny going, let alone later get witnesses to prove; I had been going to the farm alone.

He then goes on to say; "The barn is among the farm buildings marked "R" on the plan Exhibit No.1" whereas looking at the plan Exhibit No.1. It is very obvious that the barn is marked "Q" on the plan, which is one time he told the truth, however unconsciously, because that is the building I had actually taken him to find the hanky…not a sack.

In No.25. He says; whilst we were in the barn I saw a bucket containing what looked like blood stained water and a blood stained handkerchief.

Wow this guy's powers of observation are becoming beyond belief, now he can see a bucket of blood stained water, in a dark Dutch barn with the floor covered in hay or straw.

Now the interesting part is, if the water was still blood stained, it stands to reason it hadn't been there too long, yet in another statement made by Arthur Haugh, he claims he saw it in the bucket two days earlier, but I will bring that up again, after the next "claimed" statement.

No.26. On asking if the handkerchief was mine I denied it, in fact I denied it twice, maybe even thrice before the cock crowed, but I had taken him to the Farm buildings marked "Q" on the plans, where the farm office was located and the tap was beneath a night light, it also makes the sighting of the blood stained water under a light, a lot more feasible, than spotting it in a dark barn, even with a torch.

Going back to Arthur Haugh's statement, that the hanky had been in the bucket two days earlier, yet if I had denied it was my own hanky, why look for a witness to support a negative theory, that it wasn't my hanky…although they did claim they had two witnesses to say; I was in two different places at exactly the same time, ten minutes before I could have been in either of the places, which raises the question; just how many people did they persuade to tell a tiny white lie or two.

It is also worth remembering that Arthur Haugh's also found a blood stained sack, several days later in the mechanism of the combined harvester soaked in blood, that going back to No.24. Wasn't anywhere to be found or was it another red herring, as if the murderer was playing games with the police, even after I had been arrested, but I very much doubt the hankies found at the scene of the crime, had been numbered by the murderer, even if he had been at the hospital eighteen months earlier and had known the boys school number.

Also as Corby pointed out, although there was semen on the boys buttocks, he had not been penetrated…was this another red herring done before or after the murder, taking into consideration a guy has got to be really sick to murder a child anyway, even to revenge something or another, maybe a farm labourer with a grudge against the father, who was also the farmer.

In No.28. it is noted that the boys hands were tied behind his back, I am not trying to make a sick joke here, but it seems this very observant policeman who could see old boil scars on the back of my neck, but not a blood stained sock, could also see blood stained water in a dark barn, but failed to see a blood stained sock in a well lit room [but then nobody else saw it, including the doctor, that had removed my sock, to clip my toe nails] but not that the child's hands were tied behind his back, the previous evening or recalled being told by the person who had found the child, that its hands were tied behind his back, or is this another red herring, because a four year old child is not going to put up much of a struggle against a grown man and going back to the fibre from my jacket, considering he was apparently wearing mittens, that were found on the low wall next to the body.

I point this out, because during the post mortem, fibres similar to my jacket were found in one of the child's finger nails, I feel that if it wasn't planted, then it could have happened when the child grabbed my sleeve as I walked away from the boys, but he was wearing mittens, I say he was wearing them, because it is not unknown for kids to lose their mittens, even inside their homes.

Another observation being; the child had blood and sand under his finger nails, plus I apparently had a scratch [unseen by anyone other than Launders] on the back of one of my fingers, but the Blood and Sand could have come about as he struggled, because according to Dr. Clift statement; There was sand on All the child's Clothing, inside his wellingtons and on the toes of his socks, plus if the scratch had been so severe as to cause blood, that may explain why it took so long for their main witness to come forward.

Also when being examined by Dr. Menzies he makes reference to taking dirt from under my right forefinger nail, then states; there were no blood stains or injuries on my body, so no evidence to support the police, who were a greater distance away from my fingers, than the doctor's range of vision.

No.31 may not seem very important, yet on the next police statement, her name is not mentioned, in fact no one signed their name to it…Why?

Could it have been a draft copy that managed to get mixed in with the other papers or documents, but as you read through it, it becomes obvious it's been written by the same person.

The rest of the page sounds very straight forward, pointing out the channels inside the building, where I had a piss in front of two men, but had not picked up my button as it had fallen into some water…well considering the channel was 7 foot long, dropping 4 feet, there wouldn't have been any water in it anyway, in fact if a button had fallen into it, it would have gone straight down the drain.

But then we get to No.32. Quote; "We then placed a trouser button into the centre of the slaughterhouse door opening and using a hose, washed it out into the pen where the child's body had been found. The water and button drained into a water channel on the extreme northern side of the pen…" unquote.

Yet he doesn't say if he was stood still holding the hose or walking along behind the button, well I use to do high-pressure water cleaning and swept away the water using a lance, in my case 1500-2500 psi, whereas the average standing tap is 40-60 psi, but who knows in 1961 maybe farms had 80 psi taps, but I am not sure, but not "standing water taps" with 500 psi, let alone 2500 psi.

Although he does not give the dimensions of the size of the pen, he does point out the channel is at the extreme northern side of the pen! Which seems to imply it was 15-20 feet [5 to 7 yards] from the door.

Now here is a little experiment anyone can try for themselves…

Take a button [any size], place it on the ground, even if farms have rough concrete surfaces, then directing your hose at the button, then enjoy watching it whizz away from you at a great speed, for a couple of disappointing feet.

Now don't misunderstand me, I am not implying that this otherwise highly respected officer of the law, did not carry out such an experiment and he did not get the required results, all I am saying is he overlooked pointing out, that the tap was on a fire engine capable of creating 20-30,000 psi.

Because to use water to wash away dirt or grit, let alone buttons or twigs over any flattish surface, requires the person holding the hose, to have to walk along behind the object, for it to travel any distance.

Hold on a minute, he said the drain went underground and going into a manhole, which was 4 feet deep or slopped at 90% over 7 feet, so how the hell did he expect there to be a backwash, having already established that the manhole was not blocked.

Shall we call that; "34 Slight Errors" for after all; He is a highly Respectable Police Officer and god forbid, he is likely to tell deliberate lies…?

No.33. is an odd statement, about from the sand heap to the dipping pens, being of good visibility and a distance of only 50 yards.

Now why add this, except he must have written it at a later date, after securing his last minute witness at the trial.

The witness said he saw me and the child walking slowly from behind the church, holding hands towards the farm, as he was passing between two buildings inside the farm itself.

Now the only place this witness could have been, noting the good visibility of the sand heap, required being near the dipping pens, which directly points out the witness was walking to or from the slaughterhouse.

Another point, although he claimed to see me walking pass the sand heap with the boy, he did not see the girls in the sand and yet we already know that three girls were playing in there and a farm worker, observed me talking to them, as I was on my way to the farm Alone, plus when I left the girls, they had gone back to where the boys were playing and the child was not with them.

Now it is very possible that when I was seen walking from the church to the farm, the child was already dead, it is also possible I was seen walking around the farm, looking for eggs on the compost heaps, there was several compost heaps covered in straw around the farm, because looking at Exhibit No.1. There was no way anyone from that distance inside the farm could have judged where I was heading, in the next police statement it is said, I could have just walked back to the ward, unseen by anyone near the dipping pens which was immediately outside the slaughterhouse.

*   *   *   *   *

Chapter 3
Dr W V A. Erksine

Now it is possible anyone reading this chapter, without reading the rest of the book, will reach one of two conclusions, either I am paranoid or what I am about to relate, was in fact a figment of Dr Erskine's very psychologically disturbed imagination.

Dr Erskine was apparently my psychiatrist in Garlands Hospital and was obviously aware of the postulation, that not even a judge would question his evidence, without being seen to be neurotic.

Earlier in this book, I pointed out how I had been chatting to one of the policemen, when the subject of football came up, because when I had entered the ward, the football results were on the screen, and boasted that Southend never loses.

This was not said in a whisper, but more to impress everyone present, that I was from Southend, a typical 17 year olds boost, [without knowing what he was talking about] but having a need to identify himself as being from the area my family lived in, plus being repeatedly beaten up by those morons at the school, that I was not from London…okay I had lived in Ilford for some time, but that was before it got sucked into the ever expanding sewer called Greater London, but like most kids, I enjoyed sports, but not so much watching them on TV, not unlike people wearing football strips of a team, they have never watched, plus if they had asked me to name one player, I would probably have said; Stanley Matthews as he was the only one I had knowingly ever heard of…

It took another couple of years in my life, to realize that the best way to impress people, is by not trying to impress anyone…but hey I was just a stupid kid seeking an identity, plus how many kids die every year, because of the stupid betting games, that start with a group of kids, picking on lone kids, by betting they can't do something and the victims, declaring they can do it, with no idea of the consequences

But I did not say whether or not they had won or lost on that day, there were a few people present at that time and probably Erskine was one of them.

In the notes in the Lord Chancellor's Office, he is described as a Registered Medical Practitioner, with whom I apparently had a conversation two days later, during the time I was being beaten up by the nurses, who required absolutely less evidence than the police took me to court with.

Oh I will digress here as it has often been asked why; I have waited so long to try to clear my name.

Well before my operation, I could not absolutely prove that being severely incontinent, was not a state of mind and regardless of all the dubious circumstantial evidence, the police tried to use against me, I was found not guilty of the crime, as such…but locked up because of the psychologically disturbed postulations of Erskine, that implied if the judge were to release me, I would still be a dangerous threat to society, on the grounds that being incontinent was conclusive evidence, I was a psychopath and would become a schizophrenic.

Also it was only after my operation, that I approached the Probation Services, in the hope of getting my medical records, I discovered that no one had ever heard of me or the Probation Officer I had seen just after discharge, plus not having had any of the conditions placed upon me, that are placed upon ex-lifers, it was then I discovered all my Probation and Medical files had disappeared, so I wrote my story to the best of my memory.

Then gave a copy to a Barrister friend of mine [unaware he was a retired barrister] who read it and the rest is in my story.

Tomorrow which will be the 16th of January 1996, I am going to Carlisle, to search the newspaper files, then return to the hospital, to see if the old buildings are still there and to retrace my footsteps, to see how long it will take to cover my journey, adding ten minutes for when I stopped to talk to people and children.

But I am digressing…back to Erskine and his statement to the court, as I do not have a copy of the one he made as a witness, this is yet another obvious straight forward statement of accounts, until read a second time, betwixt the police statement , the second of which; I will cover later.

This quote comes from the Cumberland Evening News, Thursday, May 18th 1961. Page 5; columns 3 and 4;

"Two days after the boy's body had been found Peck was interviewed by Dr. William V. A. Erskine, of Hawthorn Cottage, Great Corby, Carlisle, a consultant psychiatrist at Garlands.

Dr Erskine in evidence said he asked Peck for an account of what happened on March 4.

Peck replied that he had been playing with some children. But had left them at 4.30.p.m.

He added that a "fair haired boy" had followed him but he told him to go away.

After leaving the children Peck said he went back to the ward. This would take him about five minutes.

Dr. Erskine said the accused had told him he was interested in the result of the Southend football match and had seen it on the television when he went into the ward.

"I asked him if Southend had won." Said Dr Erskine, "and he replied Yes." He did not say it very clearly and I asked him again. He said quite distinctly the second time I asked him "Yes."

End of quote.

Now that sounds very straight forward, any moron can see that, but wait only a moron will never question a psychologist, even Freud pointed that out, but for those who have not started to question the postulations of psychology, here are a few eye openers, to help you see more clearly.

Note he wasn't just a psychiatrist, but a Registered Medical Practitioner, thus a person greatly respected, in fact he was an authoritive voice at the hospital and who questions those in authority, and don't we All Respect the Reality, That Some People will Always Be Beyond Question! For after all is said and done; "Aren't they Gods in mortal garb?"

Although I have this faint suspicion that a lot of people reading this book have started asking themselves, just what makes such freaks, claim, "To be Perfection Itself!"

How can I prove this conversation or interview, never took place?

As you have already read the last two chapters, the chances are a few doubts are already shadowing your minds, maybe You have already returned to the last chapter and discovered one or two slight discrepancies already.

It seems I had implied; That I had been with the children until 4.30 p.m.

I had gone to see the children very briefly to tell them; I would see them the next morning to make bows and arrows, but the police claim I had said several times, that I walked with the boy as far as the laundry, at 4.30 pm. So why tell a doctor a different story.

I still feel he was present when I was examined on the Saturday night, with as many distinguished titles as he had after his name, it should be seen as a matter of course, and that such an important person would be present.

Okay that was so small or may have been misquoted by the press, which isn't uncommon for the press to do.

"He added that a 'fair haired boy' had followed him, but he told him to go away…"

The quotation signs around "fair haired boy" are actually in the paper, as if to emphasize, that at the coroner's investigation, it was discovered that the boy had "Blonde or Fair Hair" but I did not know this at the time, even throughout the statements of Launder's, I had repeatedly referred to the boy, only as the "Ginger haired boy!"

He had obviously made it his business to discover who the child was, but it is obvious that during his chat with the police, they had only made reference to the child having "fair hair" and probably forgot to point out to him; I did not know and had been talking only about a ginger haired boy.

Okay so you may exclaim; "What a pathetic excuse, so what does having fair hair prove, not that the interview never took place!" But read the next statement before screeching, because all the way through it, I refer to a ginger haired boy! Why say 2 days earlier it was a ginger boy, then tell the doctor it was fair, then an hour later during the police interview, revert to calling him a Ginger Haired Boy?

Not once did I refer to the child as being anything other than ginger, so he obviously knew something, I didn't and then claimed I told him, during a chat he imagined having with me.

In his statement it will be read, I was still claiming to have left him at the laundry, the doctor suggested I said; "This would take about five minutes" well a doctor at the hospital, would have known it was only 100 yards from the laundry to the ward, maybe just over a minute or five if walking backwards on my hands.

Okay some of you are still no closer, but for those of you who are aware that it's not a gun you worry about, but if the bullets are being aimed at you…I then claimed I was interested in the result of a football match, if I had been an avid fan, I would have been depressed, that my team had just lost, but it was just an observation of what was on the TV, whilst waiting for my program to come on, if you sit down to watch a film, before the end of the previous program, do you absorb all that information or do you concentrate on what you are interested in, come to that how many times do you study the credits after a film, has been on.

I am sure I was not and probably never will be the only person, to sit and watch a boring program, without absorbing any information other than it was on before the program you are waiting to see.

Come to think about it, I have sat down and watched a film with someone, then during the discussion afterwards, I realised; that one of us had watched a completely different film, than had just been shown.

I doubt if a street researcher, trying to discover anyone who can recount the adverts that came on, before, during and after last night's film, unless one stayed in their mind, but one out of how many adverts during a film.

I was sitting there, having rushed my tea [which must have taken me five minutes, putting me on the ward at about 4.25 p.m.] so that no one would nick the seat, before the Lone Ranger came on.

Another thing to take into consideration from the police statements is, I told them, I had seen the type-writer thing on the screen, as I approached the TV, making it approximately 4.30 p.m. 15 minutes before the nurse saw me on the ward at 4.45 p.m.....11 minutes before the result at 4.41 p.m.

Now if we were to go back to Launders statement, just prior to No.21. it will be read; "He then went into Ward B, typewriter with football results on TV." adding; "He then watched the following programmes on TV."

Okay he failed to report what the other programmes were, but it seems to add more strength to the fact, that after pointing out the type-writer, that a chat would come up about football and had that been so, he would have realised I knew nothing about football, except the positions, having played a lot of football at school.

So if the football results hadn't come up two nights before, why did this eminent doctor react to the results, when they came into his imagined conversation?

It must also be taken for granted according to his statement to the court, that throughout the conversation, I had been speaking fluently, but when asked about the football results I started to mumble, so much so he was forced to repeat the question, but did not point out, why he couldn't figure out the difference between a mumbled Yes! Or a mumbled No!. Or why they would sound both the same, hence having to repeat the question a second time.

Yet he didn't repeat any of his questions that were obviously invented of facts unknown to me at the time of his interview, i.e. the boy having fair hair, playing with the children until 4.30 p.m. or then leaving the child at the laundry at 4.30.p.m.

Doesn't it seem just slightly odd, that when making these otherwise unknown comments, I had spoken openly and precisely without mumbling, regardless of the implication that; if I had left the boy at the laundry at 4.30 p.m. and had left all the children at 4.30 p.m. then I must have been playing with all the children at the laundry until 4.30 p.m.

Note how I had failed to point out to him that I had not been playing with the children, during the afternoon, until 4.30 p.m. which is also what the police implied a couple of times, I had a visitor during the afternoon, then delivered a trifle to a ward, then stopped for a few moments in passing, to talk to the kids, regardless of having been seen talking to the girls at 4.15 p.m.

Well it was probably earlier I was speaking to the boys, considering the women's ward was less than 50 yds. from the bus stop and more or less to the boys, so by 4.10 p.m. I would be behind the church filling in the holes, with a witness to say that I was on my own, before going to chat to the girls and being observed talking to the girls on my own.

Had I forgotten so many details from the doctors interview and only recalled them again during the second police interview or maybe the police pointed out, that as far as they were concerned, I had played with the boys all the afternoon, left them to go into my ward, fifty yards away that would take 5 minutes, walking backwards on my hands.

It will also be noted that in the next statement that the police had already interviewed the girls, although it was also implied they discovered this for themselves, and it was already known by the police, that after talking to the girls, I had gone to the farm on my own, arriving back on my ward before 4.30.p.m.

Neither here nor there? Well let's return to the football results, everyone who watched TV. in those days, must have known the telecaster proceeded the results, but I had only been on that ward two weeks, that would have been my second Saturday, think about it this way, I was in an Approved School where we did not have TV's, before that in a remand centre and prior to that various hostels and houses, I never hardly ever saw a TV.

Something has only just occurred to me about the telecaster being on, as I had told the police I had seen it, that must have been an important bit of evidence, because how would I have known the program started that way, if I hadn't seen it at the time, note this was said to the police 5 hours later, it was still fresh in my mind.

Then the doctor states, he asked if Southend had won and I said yes…but why?

Think about it this way, If the football results were so crucial for an alibi and it hadn't come up in a previous conversation, then when it was possible to discover the results in the Sunday papers, why didn't I just say no or point out who they had been playing. Which had it been a genuine conversation, he would have pointed out that two nights previously I had boasted Southend Never Loses, in front of half a dozen witnesses, himself included.

Maybe I am overlooking a small detail here, which will be obvious to everyone, when I do the quotes on psychiatrist reports on me, at the time I was bordering onto schizophrenia, caused by incontinence, so maybe he had been talking to my super ego, which refused to tell me afterwards.

The next police statement will prove how deeply I had been slotted into the realms of lunacy by the police, so who would question what; "They wanted to hear" from a doctor trying to impress himself.

Yet again I ask the question, why should I have changed so many details during the chat with the doctor, from that which I had told the police, two nights earlier and then revert yet again, less than an hour after talking to the doctor, in which I had apparently been playing all the afternoon with the kids until 4.30 p.m. or how it takes five minutes to walk from opposite the church to my ward, then revert again to saying the boys hair was ginger.

All very strange and vaguely suspect to me, but then I know the interview never took place!

But no one, not even a self-respecting Q.C's or Judges, would make it obvious to a psychologist, they had no idea what he was talking about, but being highly intellectual can accept every word without question, so what chance did the jury of everyday folk have, when confronted by such an awesome pillar of Authority.

Well that should be the end of this chapter…But!

On the same page as the above quotation is the statement of the Approved Schools Headmaster, in which he paints a picture of me, that would convince any [easily convinced] psychiatrist, judge and jury, just how questionably insane I was, before being admitted to the hospital .

Earlier in the book I explained; how I was given the option of jumping off the parapet or being gang raped in the approved school, well this is the headmaster's version and afterwards I will copy out what various people had written about me, which appeared in the judges report…some of those Top Secret things, the public are not officially allowed access to for 75 years or until 2036, when I reach the age of 92, if I live that long and cannot be suggested as being too senile to remember any of the exact details, for the Home Office's benefit.

Not that I am suggesting that it is anything unusual, to have a 75 year ban on access by the public to my files, I am sure it must happen all the time, except in those rare occasions when 30-50 year bans are in order, i.e. Top Security War Crimes Secrets or Churchill's diaries or innocent hanging victims…Well that is a simple enough thing to understand, the Home Office protecting society, by refusing to let any living relative of the victims of British Justice, expose the Truth in the Home Secretaries own life span, in case it causes the unquestionable members of authority, to get red faces and be removed from the right hand of God!

Now not being allowed to prove myself innocent of that crime, until I reach 92 years of age, seems like a very fair Act of British Justice, that obviously shines so brightly as any other star in the Heavens, so much so, even 3 Wise Men would know, just how protectively Our Government Embraces; The Bill of Human Rights…"nudge, nudge, say no more, Squire!"

The Headmasters statement to the court:

"The Headmaster of Edmond Castle School, Mr J Saul, told the Cumberland Assizes at Carlisle yesterday, why he sent a youth from the school to Garlands Mental Hospital.

Mr Saul said that he sent Peck to Garlands for an examination by a psychiatrist, with a view to his admission as a patient if possible, because of the youth's peculiar behaviour at the school.

When Peck arrived from a classified school certain information and recommendations came with him.

He would be sitting in his House Room when he would suddenly clasp his head in his hands, run out into the grounds and be quite on his own for some time. The staff spoke quietly to him about these happenings, but he did not seem to remember anything about them.

The final event which led him going to Garlands was when he smashed a window to get back into the school dormitory.

The pyjamas had been given out, but Peck's were not on his bed in the dormitory so he went down to the sewing room to get them. The pyjamas were brought up as he was going down and they crossed on the way.

Another boy, for a lark opened the balcony window and put them out on the balcony, when Peck came back and eventually found them he opened the window and got out onto the balcony to get them.

Another boy closed the window behind him, locking him out. He immediately took a broom handle and smashed down the whole of the window to get in. When a member of the staff saw him he was in a very distressed state in deed, said Mr Soul." End of quote.

*   *   *   *   *

I will cover the "certain information and recommendations that accompanied me to the school" later, well I have earlier pointed out the incident of the window, [which was written in this book a few years ago] before coming across this newspaper item, which sounds all very reasonable, boys will be boys and always larking around, except on this occasion they played the joke on the schools psychopath, otherwise why else would he grab a broom handle and smash down a whole window?

But there was one small point that should have been explained by Mr Saul; where did the broom handle come from? Were the brooms usually kept on the balcony or maybe it was grabbed off an old hag who was just flying past at the time, maybe it materialized in a long slender hand, to destroy all the Vacuum Cleaners in Fair England.

The broom cupboard was outside the dormitory, so was he implying I have very long arms, whereas I had grabbed it off one of the boys, who was trying to force me to jump over the parapet and onto the stone slabs, quite a long way down, so what with the "certain information and recommendations from the classified school" it would have all been brushed smugly under the carpet, as "An only to be expected suicide, from an obviously neurotic boy!"

He also failed to point out that members of the staff did not frequent the House Rooms, except to check they were clean and just before sending the boys to bed, plus that incident took place sometime before being sent for observation and he did not explain why I was given the Job as staff boy, after being repeatedly beaten up by idiots who could not accept Southend was not in London, resulting in large bruised lumps all over my head and face,[pretty much like when I lived with a step mother, who had used lumps of wood or high heeled shoes, to beat me unconscious whenever I wet the bed] plus having a fractured skull that in very cold weather would cause me a great deal of headaches [they still do if I forget to wear a hat in winter, in fact I am sure there are a lot of people living in Northern England, can vouch for the fact; It gets very cold up there in the winter.

*   *   *   *   *

Now just what was to be found within these "certain information and recommendations" that had accompanied me to the school?

Now as they say before some news programs and radio plays, the following may contain certain information that may offend or disturb the listener, but in this case, they may offend those who consider Official Secrets Reports should be respected as such, for after all aren't Official Secrets to protect those who made then in strictest confidence, that no one will ever read them: "During their Life Time!"

Wow does this not give a hint to the authors, that if they fancy adding a little embroidery, to impress anyone stupid enough to read them as gospel, add a few pretty colours and if in doubt; make the rest up as you go along or plagiarise from other available statements, because Your Words of Authority will Never Be Questioned, then as an added sweetener, You can rest assured that whatever crap you invent, will be given "Top Priority" under the Official Secrets Acts!"

For those of you with squeamish tummy's, skip the rest of this chapter, but as those people will probably be students of psychology, who have come across too much Truth, they probably gave up reading this book long ago, to seek comfort in the delusions of normality, because the nicest part being normal, is you are never expected to question your Superiors , who have taught us for years, that to become a Perfect Model of Society, is to just accept all the crap blindly and Never Question the Words of God, omitting to point out that when people question those in Authority, they are not questioning God, but those; who in refusing to be questioned, have bestowed upon themselves; The Status of Gods…not unlike Christians who are not allowed to question the bible…

But yet again I digress

These reports I am about to copy out, are from a copy given to the judge at my trial, I suppose they are given to judges at all trials, with maybe past convictions, they were not all read out in court, but enough is said in court to verify the validity of them.

I will put an asterix after each statement and add my own comments, rather than doing the whole in one go and then expect you, to go back to each to grasp any later comments.

*   *   *   *   *

Social History
Dr Barnardo's [undated]

> "The Educational Psychologist 28/9/58. " [After discussing my intelligence scores, adds] "I found no evidence of emotional disturbances, which is strange when his case history is considered." On the 5th June he stole a tent and his housemaster reported: He has stolen several times and is not to be trusted. When questioned Peck lies about everything, he doesn't seem able to leave anything alone lately and appears to have a hold over the smaller boys here."

*Comment I brought the tent and a track bike from another boy and the "Hold" I had over the younger children, was merely that I looked after them when they arrived, usually as orphans or after being victims of violence from adults, so it was natural for them to seek friendship with an adopted older brother, than to ask questions of the staff, as one adult is pretty much like another…at least I understood that much as a kid.

They were in strange surroundings, some had never had new clothes, slept in their own bed or had a decent meal at a table, I helped them make their beds, show them their wardrobes and explained what they were for and would probably be in charge when we went playing over at Fairlop Sandpits.

Okay so I had some kind of hold over the boys, we all have some sort of control over children, if they trust us, not trust in being an adult, but when they realize You Respect Them as Human Beings and will talk to them, with lots of space for them to ask questions, such as what a word means.

I use to have a very beautiful niece; until she became a born again Christian and I had an argument with her father, about selling her soul to the devil, after refusing to invite me to her wedding, knowing Natasha really wanted me to be there, but then like any other Born Again idiot, he only told her half the facts, like my refusing to sleep with his wife in exchange for some favours, when all he needed to do was ask for a favour, but every Saturday night he would bring some guy home to satisfy/sell his wife in exchange for favours, maybe the knowledge that she didn't like the idea, turned him on [not unlike a lot of other freaks] okay I am sorry, but Jean had treated me with respect most of my life, so I wasn't interested in her as a sex object.

Anyway I was talking about my niece Natasha Brown, who helped me so much when I was trying to adjust to being in society, by explaining to me things, I was too embarrassed to ask of an adult, having been put down too many times, for not knowing what a child should know!

I had only recently been discharged and was learning from scratch, we had this really close relationship, she was 7 years old and I was 34 years old, but spiritually we were Equals, we were adults when she wanted to know something important or we were kids, when she wanted a kid to play with and for years afterwards, I referred to those years, as when we were kids together, but there were many occasions when she would take me to one side, to seek advice about what her parents had asked her to do, because my opinion was important to her.

I never lied to her, [okay I misled her to heighten a surprise] I Respected Her a Great Deal, regardless of her being my step-sisters daughter, not even related to me by blood, but we had this Special Bond, it felt as if she were my own child and was for her the uncle I wished I had had, fortunately for her, I am a bit eccentric… a bit like the uncle in; "Swallows and Amazons" and God gave me a gift of being able to break down my academic levels of speech, to those of a child, who wishes to communicate in an intelligent way and as I was experiencing for the first times, what most people take for granted and ignore or place below their levels of superiority to kids.

i.e. some adults will never go over to the park in the middle of the night, to play on the swings [very good for helping a person to relax, during stress, especially with the risqué factor thrown in], but in daylight, no one batters an eye-lid if you're going with your kids and a swing is vacant, but how many parents go to parks solely for the kids benefit and to make them happy or people after watching a ballet and are stoned by the whole experience and sometimes the colours of the costumes, but then you get the nerds who see a slight fleeting stagger of that appalling dancer, when I took her to her first ballet , I showed her a seat whilst claiming I had to see a friend, then waited for the bell and walked in and she begged me to let her see some more, so I handed her a program as a part of her Birthday Surprise and every birthday, whatever she had shown a desire to see, we would go, but she always fell for the broad hints, that had nothing to do with her surprise.

Yet I also discovered the one thing kids are better at than most adults, in so far as if I made a slight error with children, it is okay and not only that she gave me confidence, just by being confident in me.

Whenever she asked me about natural things or events, I never said to her; Oh you will understand when you are a bit older…which usually means, don't ask me questions, that I don't know how to explain the answers to, just respect me as your elder and whatever stupidity I come out with; You must accept only as being the Complete Truth of Someone In Authority!

Almost all the local kids liked me, except those in her class at school, because whenever they had a special visitor to the school, she always put her hand up to point out that she had or was about to go there with me, when the guide dog owner visited, her uncle had loads of friends with guide dogs, she had been to see plays in London, visited most of the museums and art galleries, then one day on sports day, all these kids came over to me, asked if I was her uncle and then said they All hate me, oh yeah I also taught her how to banter…snag being she'd get told off by her parents, due in part to no one holding up a board saying; "laugh" or "clap" I feel it was her 18th Birthday that sparks flew between me and her parents, there was thick snow on the ground, all the roads were impassable, but I turned up with a big gateaux and a bottle of champagne , I feel her parents prayed all night for snow, as there wasn't any festive food in the house, for her friends who couldn't make it, then after tea, I took out a jewellery box with a gold bracelet and necklace and through clenched teeth, her parents told her how lucky she was, as envy drooled from their mouths [it should be noted I often gave her parents gifts as well], then I asked her if she would say whether or not our friendship had been genuine, to which she hugged and kissed me saying yes, yes, yes, so I picked up the trinkets, gave them to her mother, then produced genuine gold jewellery, that side by side, made the 50p trinkets look like the rubbish they were, but then it was hard to tell the rubbish from gold until side by side, she went off to college and I was made to feel like an unwanted door to door salesman, whenever I called in to see them and the other kids.

I think I have really digressed this time, but I am still more or less the same person, I have been all my life, a bit of a Peter Pan I suppose, but then I still have vivid memories from my childhood, so if I can give them happy memories, it helps to subdue [if not destroy] some of my own.

*   *   *   *   *

Back to Barnardo's quote: He seems to be indifferent to advice and appears to have no deep affection for anyone; he lacks enthusiasm for work and has no interest in clubs or hobbies."

*I suppose he had misplaced my files, in which I did athletics, cross country running, swimming, collecting stamps, chewing gum cards, match boxes, which I suppose didn't leave me much time for hobbies, plus being put into another home, assured it was a naval training school, would make any kid think twice before showing an interest in anything, from an adults point of view, who I only saw at meal times or bed times…maybe it's the kids that fail society, instead of disinterested society, that are failing kids…oh yeah I was in the school choir [about the only class I turned up for], but you would think a housemaster would be a lot more observant to kids in his care and over a couple of years, plus all the reports from other homes, knowing they had arrived as battered kids, then put the blame on the kids, if the kids are unable to trust them…I know no one in our cottage went anywhere with the housemaster, unlike the kids in the other cottages, who often invited me along to events or long cross country walks…so how did he reach his twisted observation, that I was obviously disturbed, who knows he may have put all the kids in that bracket…or could it be that being incontinent, it was only to be expected that such kids were disturbed and he had probably scored top marks in his child psychology exams on child welfare.

It must be like someone who was once bitten by a dog as a child, they grow up to be terrified of dogs, with a phobia about nice dogs, evil dogs, toy dogs and dead and stuffed dogs, they accept all dogs are from the pits of hell and everyone laughs at them and suggest knowingly that the person is psychologically disturbed, even people with only the half a brain needed to study psychology, reach that conclusions…unless of course they were also savaged by a dog when they were kids.

It's based on Logic, which is referred to as psychology, but less often in its realistic reality of being Pure Evil, because evil can always justify itself and only evil people enjoy destroying innocent people's lives, if they deny wanting to indulge in sexual acts with their parents or children, which is perfectly acceptable in well balanced normal people of the ilk needed to create social workers…well versed in child psychology.

Yet again I apologise for digressing, so I will tighten this up in case it turns out like the rest of the book …

"It is regrettable that despite all that we have tried to do for him, he has deteriorated and one gets the impression that he needs to be in a place where he can get closer supervision."

*Now Dr Barnardo's not only had its own approved schools and remember, I was always apparently lying, stealing and could never be trusted…but it also had apprenticeship schools, for printing and bricklaying etcetera, so that when kids left at 18 years old they had good qualifications to start life, outside.

Well I suppose I would have had to have to have committed two crimes to have gone to an approved school, but hang on wasn't I always lying and stealing? Which I was not sent to, not even for closer observation, nor did I go to the apprenticeship school.

No…they had this much better idea, that only a person of; A Very High Level of Intelligence, which is a demanded requirement found in most Authoritive Experts could have reached as a solution, to someone obviously in need of close supervision…

They told me one day to pack my bags, refused me permission to say Goodbye to at least one friend and stuck me miles away in a hostel, where I knew no one and was told; "This is Reality, Get on with It!"

Years later whilst in Broadmoor, they introduced me to another ex-boy called Allen Sparks, a really nice guy who visited me often, with his daughter Megan, he was a printer [?]at Honeywell, and gave me my first Dictionary and Thesaurus and explained how to use it and I gave him amongst other things, manuals on all forms of advertising from a very big commercial printing company, just before I was discharged he gave me his new address in Belgium, but someone stole my address book, to track me down, because I had been the only person to be nice to him, so I wrote to his daughters friend for help, no reply, then to his companies office, then Barnardo's who refused point blank to even acknowledge he existed, regardless of the fact the person I asked, was the guy who had introduced us.

Dane's School Ilford; "Indifferent—Persistent truancy and running away from the Homes, especially when entrusted with dinner money. Was just a nuisance at school, truancy and indifferent to work"

* Obviously someone who liked to repeat himself, no wonder he was in a school for losers and anyway how would anyone want to go to a school that insisted that every morning, the kids had to repeat their two times tables and every class was done in dictation!

Yet they failed to point out, I took second prize in a National Writing Competition for Cadbury's Easter Eggs [maybe in the Archives, they still have the results for 1959], I had only failed to win First Prize, due to my bad hand-writing and smudges, I spent hours in the School Library and the local library, looking up every historical facts about Easter Eggs, I was also in the school choir, the only class I always turned up for [if not on a walk-about] and when in warm weather, when I didn't need to leave the classroom so often [if allowed, which the teachers found it funny not to let me do, so if I wet myself, they would cane me], I was in the cross-country team, having over the years of having to out run all the other kids trying to beat me up, after the teachers had refused to let me leave the room and caned me as I had to let go of myself in agony, so I had developed a good running technique both in distance and in sprints.

Oh okay I didn't spend much time in school, but I wasn't dim, due to having a retentive memory of everything I had copied out, but almost every school I went to I was given 6 of the Best several times a day, then got caned again when getting home for bringing down the Homes Good Name, but not being as dim as all the reports on me seem to imply, I had figured out, that not going to school reduced my punishments to only twice a day.

The dinner money wasn't exactly seen as theft, after all it was for my dinners, but it came in handy when my best friend and I had saved up our pocket money to go off on an adventure, to Brighton, Southend or somewhere just as exciting… which is referred to as running away, also taking into consideration that on return we were given the choice between writing out the longest Psalm, that took days between chores, with no deserts at dinner or going out to play or Six of the Best, that was over instantly, which if I stayed away a week, was better than being caned several times a day during a school week.

Dr Greenberg S.M.O. Essex County Council. 15.2.60.

> "Malcolm is obviously a seriously maladjusted boy. He is very depressed and is suspicious and inhibited that it is almost impossible to form a good relationship with him. Any "Primitive"

measures in his case are likely to be inefficient and indeed will only confirm him in his ideas of rejection and unworthiness and hence make him even more anti-social."

*It was also overlooked that since leaving Barnardo's 7 months earlier, I had 3 jobs, which were changed only because, I had been moved to three different hostels, I had got on well with the people I worked with and had spent hours over at Wanstead Ponds fishing at the weekends [I wonder how my friends felt, when I disappeared without warning after making plans together], with friends I made quite easily of my own age group at work, most of which were as a grocery delivery boy or a messenger for British Rail, meant I was in constant contact with members of society of all ages, I was adjusting quite well on my own, without their interference.

Until I was taken to court for stealing back my own money from another lodger and put into a remand home and then into a mental hospital for refusing to be adopted by someone who wanted a boy to love, well when I was 15 years old Love only meant fear, violence and pain to me, having been repeatedly told that the reason for the beatings; was because my attackers loved me.

Boyles Court Remand Home: "He is peculiar in manner and speech and has sought acceptance by the other boys by acting the buffoon, he is immature inadequate and disturbed."

*Were they being original or had they read my files, but then I was with boys of my own age and had spent some time in society and a lot of comedians, became such as a passive defence mechanism against bullies.

A report to Juvenile Court by: A Child Care Officer 23.11.60.

"I respectfully suggest to the court, the boy will require residential treatment for a prolonged period, in order to give him the necessary support to overcome the unfortunate experiences of his early life. He does not seem to realise the seriousness of the charge against him."

*This was the time I was in a remand home, for defending myself from being raped, by another lodger [highly respected by his peers], who claimed I was having a nightmare, as he forced himself into me.

It sounds as if I must have been a cupid look-a-like as a teenager, but in a photograph from that period, I look almost retarded…in retrospect if I had entertained the buggery, there is a good possibility, my life would not have become so buggered-up!

Oh the conclusion to this report was being sentenced to 3 years in an Approved School, which must enhance just how compassionate the magistrate must have been, to respond to the suggestion; Of residential treatment for a prolonged period to overcome the unfortunate experiences of his early life, especially when not allowed to explain, why I had been forced to defend myself.

But then it was a report of a "Child Care Officer" who must have been fully aware of the consequences, especially when adding; "He does not appear to realize the seriousness of the charge against him."

The Royal Philanthropy Association Classification School. 5.12.60.

"A boy of above average intelligence [though not superior intelligence], whose attitude to work is seriously hampered by his feelings of insecurity and inadequacy."

It should be noted that not one of those experts, had first-hand knowledge of observing me at a work place , I had never been sacked from a job, just moved on to another location on the whims of experts, that appear to repeat what others of their ilk had suggested, without an original thought of their own.

*Well having read those proceeding reports, as well as having gone through what I had already experienced, is it any wonder I should have given the impression of feeling insecure, let alone inadequate!

Note: although these comments are underlined by the Judge at the Murder Trial, it was also stated in many statements that although above average intelligence, his basic levels of subjects and schooling, are at the 10-12 years age level.

Dr Clarke 7.12.60. "He shows some neurotic traits, bed wetting still persist every other day, there is a speech defect and he has nightmares of an insecurity type, he had fears of the dark when younger."

*Take note of the above; Parents of all young children! If your child has fears of the dark, let alone nightmares and wet their beds, it is because they are neurotic and should be locked away from society for long periods of observation!

"On examination he is tense, anxious and restless, looking very depressed and defeated with a furrowed brow, tending to be a little paranoid, he sits and picks his fingers, he is immature and an inadequate boy, he has a poor capacity for forming emotional relationships, tending to keep to himself and not trusting adults."

*Wow, what on earth was I supposed to be doing, jumping up and down with glee, for having been sent to the other end of the country, for defending myself from a highly respectable sexual pervert, which would hardly be the best reason in the world to have an unquestionable trust in adults, which between the Homes and Remand Homes, I had been on the point of forming.

But the classic in the above statements is his scientific observation, that I had a poor capacity for forming emotional relationships...I was in an All Boys Approved School, plus constantly being beaten up, because to those idiots, Southend on Sea was in South London!

What was I supposed to have said to him, I am madly in love with a big handsome guy, who buys me flowers and chocolates, for secret kisses in the back seats of the cinema, on Saturday afternoons in Carlisle?

He obviously had only read previous reports and not asked if I had made any close friends, one of whom was to become my best friend for the next 14 years; Phil Brew, who I met again in Prison and yet again in Broadmoor and he was almost directly the reason, why I made my mock confession, to a crime I was expected to incriminate myself in, to get out of Broadmoor, when he was apparently found hanging from a bar, less than two feet above the floor.

He goes on to say: "This is a severe and emotional disturbance, there is no true evidence of psychosis at present, but then it doesn't mean to say, that he couldn't develop into a schizophrenic at a later date, the other alternative is that he may become an inadequate psychopath."

*Now what would a judge make of such a statement? Implying I am not a schizophrenic, but that doesn't mean without stretching the imagination he could become one, let alone implying I could become psychotic, a schizophrenic and an inadequate psychopath.

Why not add; "Whereas on the other hand, I could become a High Court Judge or a direct messenger between men and God or better still all paedophiles will drop dead, if I were within 100 miles of them…but come to think of it, if that were true, there would be a lot of child care experts and judges running scared…until they could figure out how to retaliate.

So there I am charged with murder of a child, and the judge reads the words, psychosis, schizophrenic and psychopath, let alone an inadequate psychopath, with those words glaring at him,

I would probably have been given a life sentence for wearing men's clothing in the privacy of my own home, with the light switched off!

Oh I am forgetting: "An Inadequate Psychopath " is exactly as it reads, It means a person who is incapable of becoming a psychopath…or as it was pointed out to me in Broadmoor as; An Intellectual Eccentric…the hair line between genius and insanity…but too easy going to become a genius or too laid back to become insane…which seems like a good idea for locking such people up, I sometimes wonder how intelligent I may have become with good tutors, had I not been born with a bladder, that failed to disconnect just prior to birth.

Is it any wonder my files have been placed under a 75 year ban from access to the public or to quote Nicholas Baker, Parliamentary Under Secretary of State, own words;

"…this is by no means uncommon with prisoners personal files as they often contain medical and welfare reports which have been written in confidence and which could not be opened for inspection without compromising the confidentiality of both author and the subject."

Well in all confidence "I am the subject" and the only comprehension I am suffering with, is that I may be just the tip of a giant iceberg, but then as those freaks are claimed to be "Experts" then what harm can it do to them, to have such great scientific discoveries that should be rewarded with the Nobel Peace Prize for their great knowledge's: That will enhance with Compassion the Future of Humanity, in the same humane ways Hitler solved the mass unemployment of the 1930' or gassing people who had subconscious desire to rape their parents and children, which seems to imply, anyone promoting such sicknesses, obviously had a subconscious desire to be exterminated! He just didn't realize just how many Heads of State, came into the world via incest.

Which may explain why those dubious "Experts" wish to remain anonymous during their lifetimes?

Cynical? Who Me? Never!

But yet again I digressed.

Runwell Hospital 7.3.60. "I.Q. W.I.S.C. Verbal scale 116, Performance scale I.Q. 125. Full scale I.Q. 123 above average."

*Not bad having a verbal scale of 116, considering I use to apparently mumble a lot, in fact I still sort of do, when forgetting to carry on a sentence, before reverting to other thoughts or trying to avoid something that will conjure up a memory, I would rather not stay in, from a time to be forgotten. Okay my I.Q.rating went up a lot more higher by the time I got to Broadmoor, but considering I had very little schooling and less encouragement, plus more than enough blows to my head, I suppose an I.Q. of 123 at 16 years old, wasn't all that bad, but this guy gave a fair and fairly observant report, possibly because I saw him more than Once!

His notes: "Unable to communicate freely. Feels unhappy when others pick on him. With psychiatrist was shy at first, but as they progressed he talked freely with warmth of feeling. Described as solitary and suspicious, no evidence of mental decease, adjusted well, left to work on a farm."

*The above was written when I was sent to a mental hospital for refusing to be adopted by a family in Kent, with my family living in Essex, isn't it a strange comment to observe, that a kid put into a nut house, for refusing foster parents [most of whom only wanting to adopt kids older than 14, who will become an extra pay packet], should appear to be solitary and suspicious or felt unhappy when a lot of psychologically disturbed men picked on him, but let's not overlook how once someone gained his confidence, how he expressed himself with warmth of feeling and showed no signs of mental disease, to someone who had a lot more contact with mental patients, than any of the other child welfare workers or casual observers above!

It should also be observed that this report was written, 3 weeks after the one by Dr Greenberg. S.M.O. Essex, County Council. 15.2.60.

Also during that stay in Runwell, I met a friendly nurse, who took me to Battlesbridge fishing and I was given the job of washing the Hospitals Fire-Engine, so I had some friends who were adults, pretty much like I am today, I have a lot of teenage friends that trust me and seek my advice, because I treat them with Respect!

This next one is odd, in so far as it was written 10 days, before the trial started…

Report from P J Quinn M.R.C.P.I. D.P.N. Deputy Superintendent, Saint Nicolas Hospital, Gosport. 10.5.61.

"He is mentally alert and fully appreciates the seriousness in which he finds himself."

*Lying bastard, I had no idea how serious the case was going to become, still convinced; I could not be found guilty under British Justice, for a crime I had not committed, no one had said anything about, getting a life sentence not for murder, but for the fantasies of twisted psychiatrist, all of whom as has been discovered, quoted each other, from original sick theories of Freud and apart from the one incidence of self-defence, whilst being raped [that everyone these days knows it is a serious offence to strike a nonce, with longer sentences for the assailant, if he beats one up that is raping a child], note apart from that one act of defence, not one statement was made to imply I was or had ever shown signs of being a violent person.

"There is no suggestion of any psychotic disturbance. Intellectually he is of high average level or just above, although this is not obvious at first and is obscured by an appearance of vagueness and dullness, combined with a functional speech defect, scholastic attainments fall far below what one would expect."

*Hold on a moment, is this Dr Quinn's diagnosis or have we all read this somewhere before, almost word for word? It might explain why so many people with dubious sexual leanings become students of psychology, knowing whatever fantasies they come out with will never be questioned, by anyone except a neurotic that will be locked away from society.

"Throughout his career he has shown many neurotic and psychopathic traits; Bed wetting still persist occasionally, even now. As a child he had nightmares and says he walked in his sleep."

*Bed wetting "occasionally?" I suffered from Severe Incontinence, until I was 46 years old, then met a urologist, who although initially thought it may be in my mind, until he discovered a new reality, but he was a qualified urological surgeon , that based everything on reality and not postulations on stupid theories…but then how many witches were drowned on even less evidence.

On the other hand why hasn't a Prison Psychiatrist, written a thesis on the fact: "That All Psychopaths are Incontinent!"

Hold it, isn't that statement almost yet again, word for word, what Dr Clarke had to say on 7.12.60. five months before hand, but added I had fears of the dark.

Now how many kids [let alone adults] are there, who if not repeatedly beaten unconscious or senseless, were or still are afraid of the dark, it would seem this country has a serious problem, with such a large number of children, becoming neurotic, let alone psychopaths or schizophrenics, however inadequate!

Well at least we have found the connection, between wetting the bed and being charged with murder, because the only evidence that was given to the Judge; to prove beyond "Reasonable Doubt" as to my psychological state of mind, was the fact I wet the bed, which proved beyond a shadow of any reasonable doubts, I was obviously a neurotic psychopath!

"The reports from various people who have examined or observed him from time to time underline his instability, his incapacity to form strong or sustained emotional relationships with other people, his continual failure to or adjust to social demands for any length of time."

*Now this does deserve a digression; how on earth can any teenager be expected to form a sustained relationship, when they get moved on, the moment a friendship is being formed, let alone an emotional relationship, but I admit that I still find it hard to adjust to social demands, in so far as I rarely take it for granted that "Normal People" know what Reality Is!

"He has been described variously as untruthful, unreliable, irresponsible, untrustworthy and failing to respond to remedial measures.

To justify the opinion that there was substantial impairment of mental responsibility, Maternal deprivation, neglect, affectionless parents, illegitimacy and prolonged stay in public care are known to produce developments of the personality along psychopathic lines, although a proportion of such children are able to make a satisfactory adjustment in later adolescence."

*Is he saying that children who are put into care by the SS [social services?] stand a far greater chance of becoming psychopaths, than children who grow up in society? If this were true, then how can they explain why are there a greater number of psychopaths in mental hospitals or the dozens of SS staff in prisons, for beating and raping children in their care, let alone the large numbers of paedophiles and rapist, let alone serial killers, that are known to have grown up within the stability of a caring happy family home?

"The difference in outcome is probably due to basic genetic make-up of the individual."

*Well that should explain why the basic requirements of child social workers, is the necessity to have qualifications in Zionist psychology, as one is forced to yet again to ask the question; If there has ever been evidence of anyone being able to accept the postulations of Freud, without trying to justify, their sexual desires towards children or their parents!?

"The ultimate decision on the issue of responsibility will be a matter for the Court, and in view of the circumstances and distressing nature of the offence, the Court might demand a stronger evidence of abnormality. A successful defence on these lines would be uncertain, particularly if the Prosecution contest the plea strongly."

End of quotations.

Yet doesn't this leave us with another couple of important questions, owing to all these were the parts of Psychiatrists reports that were "underlined" by the Judge!

Let us return to the evidence read out in court, by Dr Erskine, in which I claim such an interview never took place and compare it to the statement of Dr Quinn.

Hold it, before comparing those two people, there is a slight, almost trivial question that should be asked and probably a lot of you; may have already noticed a strange little vacuum…

If Dr Erskine was my doctor at Garlands, why wasn't there a report from himself or any other doctor from Garlands Hospital, amongst the reports in the Judges copy of "My Social History?"

Now without being cynical, isn't it enough to scare anyone, knowing that such statements can be placed in front of any court, with the reassurance that such information, having been written in confidence, will be placed under an Official Secrets Act, in case the Truth may compromise the confidentiality of the author?

Almost every conclusion this very eminent Dr Quinn had reached a week before I was due to go trial, were just a lot of quotations of other reports.

There is also every possibility that such an interview also never took place or could it be simply a case of; "All Great Minds Think Alike?"

That it is to be taken for granted, that anyone who wets the bed is a psychopath or a neurotic schizophrenic and therefore obviously capable of or very likely to be guilty of murdering a child, because bed wetter's are incapable of forming any emotional relationships and everyone knows that the most distinguishing trait of a psychopath is:

To quote; Collins English Dictionary. Third Edition 1991. Page 1252.

"Psychopath. n. a person afflicted by with a personality disorder characterized by a tendency to commit antisocial and sometimes violent acts and a failure to feel guilt for such acts."

Page 1384. Schizophrenia [to quote a small part of it]:

"1. any of a group of psychotic disorders characterized by progressive deterioration of the personality, withdrawal from reality, social apathy, emotional instability etc."
Unquote.

I have no idea what is the "Most Terrifying Reality" everyone in this country to, Is it the absolute Powers of Psychologist to Destroy the lives of whoever they wish, on a whim of fantasy!

Or could it be Her Majesties Government, with its inability not only to Not Question such "Fabrics so Fine" but to offer those Psychopathic [Collins Dictionary. P.1252] Perverts, complete protection under the provisions of S.5.[4] of the 1967 Act, that will guarantee them protection from inspection without compromising the confidentially of the Author, during His or Her life time!

Not overlooking the equally "Horrendous Reality" That the people who control the lives of our children, have to have qualifications of the kind that imply: the reason why children wet their beds is; "Because they have a subconscious desire to be punished violently and without mercy by their parents, due to a guilt complex, brought about from wanting to have sex with their parents!"

Okay some people can be forgiven, for not having studied psychology and just accepting what the experts tell them, but the chances are they have never had their lives destroyed, because some sexually perverted freak, has decided they are guilty of mumbo-jumbo, rather than physical medical reality…that they prefer to ignore, plus none of you have ever searched old book shops or visited libraries to glean information, from mainly unquestionable jewish child psychologist , but then the victims of a physically curable disability, have always been brainwashed, into thinking they deserve a whole life of being humiliated and persecuted, by GP's, whenever seeking "Medical?" Help.

The chances are I wouldn't be sitting here telling the Truth of Reality, if I had never had the operation, that gave me the conclusive proof that Incontinence is not all in the victims mind, and no one will ever know how many committed suicide, after removing all the evidence of their unbearable shame, because even in death, they did not want people to discover their dirty secret!

Or murdered by the parents of those psychological freaks they had given birth to!

Don't forget Hitler did not go around arresting jews because of their religion, he only ordered the arrest of those sexual perverts, that were promoting paedophilia and it just so happened, the bulk of them turned out to be jews, who even today, refuse to recognise the hundreds of thousands of jews who grew up and lived in Germany throughout the entire war.

But yet again there are plenty of governments, that are still making it illegal to question the Jewish version of what took place, implying those camps were just to kill jews, but never explaining if that was the case, why did the camps, run by the Gestapo [most of whom were Jewish landowners], had to practice on 15,000,000 none jews before getting around to the jews who were the only survivors that then carried on persecuting bed wetting children, because of their subconscious desires to rape their parents or murdering Palestinians, on the grounds that they have sub-conscious desires to kill All Zionist Nazi's, that are protected by governments that make paedophilia a misdemeanour.

But let's not forget those bed wetting children, who became orphans, due to WW2 and/or road accidents, is it implied they are necrophilia's, that can only get turned on by dead people, but are refused work in mortuaries, just in case they get turned on, come to think about it, I have also met such men, that strangely enough, as if to prove the experts wrong, did not suffer with incontinence!

One last point of a general nature, as we have all discovered from the above reports, apart from being an inadequate psychopath, which to an uninformed judge or jury, would appear to be another form of psychopathic illness, it was repeatedly pointed out, that I was very immature, which I agree with, had the mental age of a 10-12 year old, with an above average I.Q. even though I rarely went to school.

Now when I was in prison, I noticed that most of the men that came in illiterate left illiterate, in general life most people stop their academic studies the day they leave school, the rest of their lives are covered with experiences…and many people don't learn anything from them either.

Okay this may not be being written out in an acceptable orthodox style, but I feel You will agree, that for someone suffering with so many adverse traits, that rendered me unable to make use of my intellectual abilities at 16-17 years of age, I have yet again destroyed the stupid postulations of those; "Never to be Questioned Authorities" by struggling to teach myself almost everything I know on the academic level and I have already pointed out, long before discovering these gems of Hyper intelligent morons, within 2 years of going into prison I had read every book in the library [okay a lot didn't make much sense, but I got there eventually]and in those days, prisoners were not locked up 23 hours a day and we had lots of association time, 7 a.m. to 8 p.m.

Plus during some of my digressions, I am sure You are aware of my abilities to be able to Share and Offer to people, Friends as well as Humanity, levels of Love and Compassion far in access of your; "Average Perfectly Normal People" or could it be people have misunderstood Inadequate Psychopaths, although I will admit that over the years this book has been evolving, I have suffered with a lot of depressions, because I had to force myself to relive memories of things from my childhood, I have tried for most of my life to forget.

But then at some point during the writing of this book it occurred to me, how everything in my life seemed to happen in such a strange sequence of events, that it is as if I needed to, experience all these things, to make the writing of this book possible.

Sometimes [well quite a lot of times] I can almost justify not writing any of this, but then that would involve condoning whatever has happened to myself, as being acceptable for anyone else and I do not consider my life to be unique, what has happened to me, can also happen to You, if not all of it, then a least a large part of it, even if you do not have incontinence.

Your lives are being controlled by the postulations of psychology, your children can be snatched by social services without reasons, put into homes in which they cannot escape being beaten or raped or forced to commit suicide or become sold to those freaks who make snuff movies, without any investigation, because some eminent psychologist has written a report, condemning that child as being disturbed and who is there to protect our children, when the Courts give the SS the Powers; that prevent the press investigating …Them!

Isn't it about time for a law to be passed, that requires the most basic requirements of all social workers, is to be able to read and write in English and to have brought up two level headed children, the youngest of which must be at least 17 years of age, before they can apply for the position, without any qualifications in perverted child psychology, because what such people don't know about natural child psychology, no one will ever know.

This country also claims that everyone, has a right to have access to any confidential files on themselves, those reports I came across almost by accident, well until I discovered them, I had no knowledge they existed and they could have remained forever unquestioned.

Also why is there such a tight limit in which a person can appeal, before it's taken for granted, that they have silently accepted the guilt, then forced to make a mock confession to gain freedom, then threatened to be returned for further treatment, if they try to clear their names.

Okay I know I was a bit dim during the trial and waited for my court appointed solicitor to explain things to me, but it took me years to figure out, that although I was found not guilty of the crime, but locked up to protect society from a dangerous psychopath, but then to add insult to injury, I was force via physical and psychological violence, to incriminate myself in a crime, to protect Her Majesties Government.

Okay I am still under the threat of being returned for more treatment, for a sickness I never had in the first place, but that is only if I approach the Courts of Appeal, but hopefully one day someone may publish my story and prove my only problem was in the minds of those psychologically disturbed psychiatrist, who are still free to destroy your own lives and those of your children in: "This So-called Civilized Country and Most of the World!"

*   *   *   *   *

Chapter 4
The Second Police Statement

This is the second statement the police claim was made, in the presence of Detective Superintendent Oldcorn, D/Sgt Launder, Mr Atkinson and Myself.

This is the statement that was made directly after the strange interview with Dr Erskine.

My apparent state of mind, in the minds of the police will be very apparent, from their first question.

Therefore they had more or less openly pointed out, that I was the perfect candidate for a quick result, who was going to query such an implication, especially with the notes in the previous chapter, at their disposal.

If I haven't already pointed it out, I was at the hospital under general observation, not on mind twisting drugs or any other form of therapy.

As I copy out this statement, I will number each question and reply as 1.Q. 1.R. 2 Q. 2R, etcetera, to make life a little easier later for cross-referencing.

Interview at Garlands Hospital on Monday 6th March. 1961. Commenced at 3.10 p.m. concluded 4.05 p.m.

Present; D/Superintendent Oldcorn, D/Sgt Launder, Mr Atkinson and Accused.

Position explained to Mr Atkinson by Superintendent Oldcorn and D/Sgt Launder.

1. Q: Now Malcolm you have given us one account of what happened on Saturday. You remember Saturday don't you?

1. R: Yes.

2. Q: And do you remember what you told us then.

2. R: Yes, a bit.

3. Q: Well since we last saw you we have got a bit more information that leads us to   believe that what you did say about what

you did on Saturday is not true. We have a bit more information and I will tell you about it.

(No 3.R :)

4. Q: You remember telling us that on Saturday you did see this little boy, George Warwick, do you remember that?

4. R: Yes.

5. Q: And you said you left him at half past four at the corner of the laundry, is that right?

5. R: Yes.

6. Q: Now we asked you about the stuff on your shoe and you said it was that if it was blood it was animal blood.

6. R: It could be nothing else.

7. Q: You also said you got it off the compost heap. This blood has been examined and we know that it was human blood. Have you any explanation for that being on your shoe?

7. R: No all blood is animal blood.

8. Q: Do you know how it got there.

8. R: No.

9. Q: Does that mean you didn't get it off the compost heap?

9. R: That's the only place you could get it.

10. Q: There was also human blood on your trousers. Can you explain how that got there?

10. R: I don't remember seeing it there.

11. Q: Previously Malcolm you said that the time you were in the farm was about 11 o'clock on Saturday morning.

11. R: Yes I remember afterwards that I did go in there with three or four of the other boys and I threw them up on the hay stack.

12. Q: What time was that?

12. R: I couldn't tell you. It was after dinner. They wanted me to play cowboys. I told them I was too old for it and they asked me throw them up on the hay stack.

13. Q: Which of the children were there?

13. R: There was the farmer's son and the little boy with the jeans on. One of the nurses came up in his car with his daughter to see the animals.

14. Q: Was that the nurse who is on your ward at the moment.

14. R: Yes I think it is, he has a blue car, a Hillman I think, it is not a Minx.

15. Q: Was that before Miss Dawson came?

15. R: Yes.

16. Q: What time would that be?

16. R: I couldn't tell you. Can I look out of the window to see if the car is there. He had a little girl with him about 5 or 6.

17. Q: Was that the last time You went into the yard?

17. R: Yes.

18. Q: So that I understand it You were there at 11 o'clock and you were last there just after dinner.

18. R: Yes.

19. Q: Did you do anything else when you were there with the little boys?

19. R: Yes we had a look at the bullocks and went along and saw the pig sties. The little boy couldn't see them so he stood on a barrow and then he could see.

20. Q: Which little boy was that?

20. R: The smallest one.

21. Q: Was that the little boy you left at the laundry at 4 o'clock?

21. R: I think so.

22. Q: Was that all you did when you went into the farm the second time.

22. R: We looked all round and then they asked me to help push them up. I pushed one up feet first, the other stood on my shoulders and the littlest one I just threw up like putting the shot. He didn't hurt himself because the other two boys got him up see and then I showed them the way to get down.

23. Q: That was in the barn was it Malcolm?

23. R: Yes in the Dutch barn.

24. Q: You told us, you remember the other night that you went back to the farm yard on your own for another purpose.

24. R: No that was the last time I went over with them.

25. Q: Well now Malcolm can you go through again then your movements of that afternoon. What time did Miss Dawson leave. Ten to four?

25. R: No four o'clock. The first bus comes at ten to four. There was a crowd waiting and then there was another bus come at 4 o'clock and she went on that.

26. Q: What did you do then Malcolm?

26. R: I came back to the Home to look for someone.

27. Q: Then where did you go.

27. R: I came to this entrance [indicating front door] where I saw another lady saying goodbye to her family. I went into the female ward and asked to see the sister. I must have been in about 10 minutes because they could not find the sister. I gave her this trifle sort of thing. I had to give it to the other lady who had just gone out. Then I came back to where that lady was and went pass the sweet shop towards the canteen. I walked along to where the other boys were, told them I would be back down on Sunday morning with some sticks and string to make bows and arrows. Then when I walked away two boys followed me and asked if I was going. I told them I wasn't. One boy left me across the road from the church. When I got to the laundry I started going for my tea and that would be about half past four.

28. Q: When you got into the hospital Malcolm what did you do?

28. R: I went to the toilet, went upstairs and saw the football results coming on, so I sat down and watched them.

29. Q: Was it the tele-type.

29. R: Yes.

30. Q: Who did you sit besides watching television.

30. R: I sat down besides one person. I don't know what his name is and then another came up and said; "Would you jump in my grave as quick?" I said I thought he was sitting somewhere else. Then I sat down and watched the football and that.

31. Q: We have been told that after the visitors left, you saw another patient as you were walking up towards the laundry with the little boy.

31. R: Yes I saw a German artist.

32. Q: We have been told that after the visitors left you went across to the fence round the farm yard and spoke to three girls.

32. R: You mean just behind those trees don't you. I went to fill in some holes. I had dug up some flowers for my visitor. The little girls were playing on a heap of sand behind some trees or something. They asked me if the cat had gone and I told them it had.

33. Q: Was George with you then.

33. R: No.

34. Q: Where was he?

34. R: I don't know.

35. Q: We have also been told that after speaking to the little girls you went into the farm yard with the little boy.

35. R: No I came out this side of the building.

36. Q: You know the heap of sand the girls were playing on?

36. R: Yes.

37. Q: Were you speaking to them.

37. R: Yes. It is near to the fence where the compound is. There is a compound there with two round things. One has sugar beet in it and the others got a compost heap with something in it.

38. Q: You didn't mention this to us on Saturday night Malcolm when we were asking you about your movements on that day.

38. R: I didn't think you were going to be interested in that.

39. Q: When you went up to the little girls…

39. R: I didn't go up to them. I stood about [from the door to the window] from them.

40. Q: Where was George then.

40. R: I couldn't tell you. I don't know. I think he went back to his friends. I don't know. Oh yes he had a little shovel with him, that's right. I knew he was carrying something other than a stick. It was a red one, the kind you have on the beach.

41. Q: When did he have that with him.

41. R: I think he had it with him all the afternoon.

42. Q: It is rather important Malcolm that we establish where the little boy went when you walked towards the girls. Where was the little boy then.

42. R: As far as I know he was on the road. I don't know where he was.

43. Q: Where was he when you left him?

43. R: At the Laundry.

44. Q: And did you see him again after you first left him at the laundry.

44. R: No.

45. Q: Have you any idea which way he went when you left him.

45. R: No.

46. Q: Did you yourself go into the farm after you spoke to the girls.

46. R: No.

47. Q: Exactly what time did you get this stuff on your boots off the compost heap.

47. R: I don't know.

48. Q: Well you have told us you were there twice.

48. R: Yes.

49. Q: Can you remember the times of those visits.

49. R: We had just finished a game of billiards, 11'clock; it was about elevenish and the second time between half past 12 and 1 o'clock.

50. Q: When was it you wiped your shoes.

50. R: That was in the morning.

51. Q: Why did you go on the compost heap.

51. R: To see if any more eggs where there, because I found an egg there previously and the chickens always scuffle up there.

52. Q: How long did you stay talking to the little girls.

52. R: They just asked me where the cat was and I said it would be back next Saturday because in the afternoon they had been playing with it.

53. Q: You said that the two small boys walked away with you and one went back. We have been told that you took George, you know George don't You?

53. R: No.

54. Q: The little boy in the pants you described him yourself as Kidda you called him.

54. R: The one with ginger hair?

55. Q: He went with you to the farm yard to get some sticks for a bow and arrow.

55. R: No, we were going get that in the morning. We were all going to be there at 9 o'clock except one boy who was a Catholic and he was going to be there at 10 o'clock.

56. Q: You have been in Edmond Castle. Do you get an handkerchief issued in Edmond Castle.

56. R: No I don't know.

57. Q: Each boy has a number haven't you?

57. R: Yes.

58. Q: What was your number?

58. R: 40 something. I have it on my trousers anyway.

59. Q: Forty what.

59. R: I gave my handkerchief in when I got my clothes changed. I left it upstairs because I was told I was coming back the same night.

60. Q: Where did you get your clothes changed.

60. R: They just gave me a clean shirt.

61. Q: What was your number at the school.

61. R: 40 or 41. Yes 41.

62. Q: We know it was 42. Is that right.

62. R: I don't know, I think so, yes, It was 42 that's right.

63. Q: Near to where we found this little boy's body was an Edmond Castle handkerchief with the number 42 on it.

63. R: I heard you found one of my buttons in the pig sty.

64. Q: The button was lying right next to the little boy.

64. R: It couldn't have been because I didn't lose a small button near the pig sty.

65. Q: Where did you lose your button.

65. R: I lost it when I went with two men to look at the slaughterhouse. It fell off into some water and I couldn't be bothered to look for it.

66. Q: Talking about the place where they kill the cows. Where did you lose your button.

66. R: In the drainage where the blood drains out, because the things here slopes down and the little drain comes out into the pen.

67. Q: Is that the new part of the slaughterhouse.

67. R: It is all new isn't it. It's an old building but it is in the new part. The one was out of use and they could get fined for using old equipment which was painful to animals.

68. Q: That's where you lost your button, but when did you lose your button.

68. R: Sometime last week. I'll tell you what day it was. It was the day they brought the combined harvester down.

69. Q: Who was with you in the slaughterhouse?

69. R: One of the blokes was a man who brought the combined harvester up and the other was just a foreman, he opened the door and we all marched in.

70. Q: Which button was it you lost.

70. R: One of the bottom ones.

71. Q: Your fly buttons you mean.

71. R: It has been lost for some time.

72. Q: Which button was it then.

72. R: The front trouser button.

73. Q: Were they the trousers you were wearing on Saturday.

73. R: Yes, they are the only ones I'd got.

74. Q: What you are saying is that the button was lost accidentally and the blood on your shoes was off the compost heap.

74. R: I didn't say it was off the compost. I said it was the only place it could have come from.

75. Q: And the Edmond Castle handkerchief with 42 on it can't have been yours.

75. R: Was it a white one.

76. Q: You said you left your handkerchief at the school.

76. R: I said I left one of my handkerchiefs at the school. I remember I had two. I washed one because it was dirty. One was fine material and the other course. I always keep, a course one because if you use a white one only twice its dirty.

77. Q: What happened to the course one.

77. R: I left it on the radiator.

78. Q: Is it still there.

78. R: No.

79. Q: Where is it. How did it get off the radiator.

79. R: Someone may have mistaken it for a bit of rag.

80. Q: Where did you get the string from in the farm yard.

80. R: We didn't get any string from the farm yard. We only had one bit of string and I got it from the window blind.

81. Q: Where did you intend to get your string from on Sunday morning.

81. R: I thought I had some in my locker.

82. Q: Just pay attention now. To refresh your memory. This little boy, the ginger haired little boy was found dead behind the slaughterhouse on Saturday night.

82. R: I was told he was found in the pig sty.

83. Q: A button which might have been off your trousers was near to him and a handkerchief with the number 42 on it was near to him and you have blood on your left shoe and on your trousers also your left sock. Did you have anything to do with

this boy's death.

83. R: No.

*   *   *   *   *

[A digression…due to this being copied out on a modern computer…it keeps on insisting in replacing the spelling errors and one or two annoying things…but I will keep it faithful to the original copy, plus if I figure out [or get help] how to include photocopies of printed evidence and photo's, you will be able to compare them.]

It should also be noted, that the above statement was not signed by anyone, unlike Lauder's, but the top of each page it is marked; "Exhibit 47. CID."

Now before going into details that points out too many obvious errors, I will first cover the points that leave a big question mark over the dubious interview in which the statement of Dr Erskine, claimed took place, moments before the above interview with the police.

He claimed I had referred to a; "fair haired boy", yet in the above [or any other statements, covering the colour of the boys hair] statement, no fair haired boys were referred to.

54. Q: little boy in the in the pants…kidda you called him.

54. R: The one with ginger hair?

Well apart from never ever heard the term; kidda before going into the court room, remember this statement was made on the Monday, after it was discovered by Dr Cliff and Dr Corby and made reference to in Lauder's signed statement in No. 28. that the boy had blonde or fair hair.

Yet in this interview, conducted by Lauder and Oldcorn, "They" in 82. Q; "…This little boy, the ginger haired little boy…"

Why didn't they correct me, if I had made an error or could it have been; That they had found the ginger haired boy, but as this boy had only followed me for 50 feet, not having taken in the colour of his hair at a glance, they led me to believe, that the child that had died, was the same child, I thought they were referring to.

Yet regardless of that query, it does not explain why; I should have said to the doctor; "Fair haired boy" when I didn't know a fair haired child, wasn't involved, I may never have discovered this point, if I had not found the police statements, all these years later or the newspaper articles.

Again there comes a small easily overlooked detail, [especially by the Home Office, who never for one moment, thought it possible I would ever get access to the files] pointing out I had been in the ward when the results came on, read again after R.28. which says: "I went to the toilet, went upstairs and saw the football results coming on, so I sat down and watched them" overlooking nothing was said about having my tea first, they replied;

29. Q: Was it the tele-type.

29. R: Yes.

*   *   *   *   *

Now to go further into this statement.

Everyone reading this has a definite advantage, over the Trial Jury, that being you have the "Exact Copies" of both police statements, plus Dr Cliff's and Dr Corby's report, to refer to.

So let's start with the mysteriously vanishing blood on my shoes.

We already know that wet blood was found on to toe of my sock and inside the toe of my shoe, plus some in the basket weave pattern, that looked as if it had been wiped off or should we start to presume; "It had been wiped On?"

We have nine references to Blood; "Being on the Outside of My Shoe!" The night "Before" being given to Cliff and Corby by D/Sgt Launder, the blood had fallen off; the day after my shoes had been taken away from me and given to Launder for safe keeping or forensics.

6. Q: Now we asked you about the stuff on your shoe and you said that if it was blood it was animal blood.

6. R: It could be nothing else.

7. Q: You also said you got it off the compost heap. This blood has been examined and we know that it is human blood, etc…

7. R: No. All blood is animal blood.

Okay read as it is, it may sound as if I were trying to be clever, but was that the question and answer, because if we return to Launder's statement after No.22 we read "When told that the matter on his shoe looked like blood, he said; "It looks like blood it will be cow, pig or chicken."

The wording is the way it's written in the statement, i.e. not "If it looks like blood etc. as far as I knew at that time, the blood on the heap was animal blood.

Q: 8 to R:9. Does that mean you didn't get it off the compost heap. That's the only place you could get it.

Here they digressed slightly by pointing out, the blood on my trousers, then claiming I couldn't remember seeing it there, yet in Launder's statement No.13. I had explained how it got on my trousers, plus the statement by the nurse who caused it to be on them.

Now we leap forward to Q: 47. When we return to the question of blood on my shoe, well this time it read "Boot".

Then again in Q. 50: when was it you wiped your shoe…but no mention on my hankies that I had wiped them with.

Q: 74 is this strange statement; "What you are saying is that the button was lost accidently and the blood on your shoe was off the compost heap."

How many people lose a trouser button deliberately or was it deliberately wiped clean then placed next to the child's body, it's a pity I don't have a copy of the photograph, in which it will be noticed that the area, is very wet as if it recently rained, but the button was lying on top of an open bag of dry cement powder [maybe the officer had never left an open bag of cement in a damp place, let alone rain] with just a little dust on its lower edge, but had it been next to the child's body, it would have been at least be "Dirty".

Q: 83. "…you have blood on your left shoe and on your trousers, also on your left sock."

Eight references to blood and debris from the compost heap On My Shoe, yet this was after Cliff and Corby had found no blood on the Outside of My Shoe, was this an error by two forensic scientist or was this an error on the police behalf, as they tried to convince me that the blood I was aware of being on my shoe, was human blood, which meant the child was already dead when I entered the farm and I had picked it up, somewhere away from the slaughterhouse, but what happened to the blood and straw on my shoe and why wasn't there any blood on my sock, the night I was examined?

Note at the time of the second interview they knew for a fact, that the blood had been wiped off and substituted with human blood, they were also aware of their own stupidity; in overlooking to make sure that some of the blood should have been inserted in the crevices, between the sole and the upper section of the shoe, therefore desperate to cover themselves…

Notice how the interview starts as if they took it for granted, I was an imbecile:

Q: 1. Now Malcolm you have already given us an account of what you did on Saturday. You remember Saturday don't You."

Then in Q: 3 they point out they have got a bit more information that implied I was not telling the truth.

What was this information? That the animal blood had been transplanted with human blood or was it the information gathered during their extensive investigations such as Q: 31. "We have been told…you saw another patient as you were walking towards the laundry."

Again in Q: 35. "We have been told that after speaking to the little girls you went into the farm yard [okay they added; with the little boy]"

Then yet again in Q: 53. Where I am again made to appear to be stupid: "We have been told that you took George, you know little George don't you?"

Now where on earth did they manage to get so much important information so quickly, well if we return to Launder's statement, we discover the source of all this detective work, was Myself, as I pointed out who could prove I had been alone, but twisted into suggesting I was with the boy.

The answer to Q: 31 being; yes I saw a German Artist. In Launder's statement, just prior to No.22. "He also said that a German from Ward 9 saw him with the boy." Actually I saw him near the church, after leaving the boy and I was on my own, a fact they must have discovered, otherwise they would have called him into court as a witness, they also changed O.T. to Laundry!

The answer to Q; 35. After speaking to the little girls, although for some reason it was omitted in Launder's statement, there was that very strange little comment, at the end of the statement, No.33. Quote: "The vision from the sand heap to the dipping pens is good and is about 50 yards".

The dipping pens were outside the slaughterhouse, so was this a reference to the fact that anyone entering or leaving the slaughterhouse had a perfect view for 50 yards, which is where the mystery witness must have been standing, when he claimed; he saw me walking with the boy, but failed to see the girls or the farm worker, who also saw me talking to the girls.

Whatever the reason, obviously they made a double error.

Q: 53. I had already told them that two boys followed me, one a few yards and the other at the end of the O.T. building, before crossing the road to the church to fill in some holes of plants, I had dug up for my visitor, Launder's statement No.20 leaving the boy at the church, in that statement it was implied I took them across the road to the church and one went back. In R:32 I again made reference to filling the holes behind the church.

Note how the statement started as if they were talking to someone, they had already taken for granted was an imbecile, not overlooking the by then, well known fact; I was in an Approve School for "attempted" GBH, and also in a mental hospital and probably when doubt has been thrown in someone's direction, all the slugs crawl out of the garden and add reasons to put a person down, probably the implications within my social reports.

Overlooking some had been by people, who had met and spoken to me several times and had overruled their first impressions of my being a dullard, a loner and suspicious, only to discover I had an overall I.Q. Rating of 123, with no evidence of mental decease and well adjusted.

Read through such replies as No's. 11, 14 and 19 I was acting in a quite responsible way, taking the children around a farm yard, remember I had worked on a farm and aware of most of the dangers, so must have picked the smallest child up several times to look into the stalls and sties.

In R; 22 I was throwing them up into the hay and helped them down again safely, a nutter would have just left them up there, not giving a damn about their safety.

In R:25. I was aware of the bus times and in R:27. Gave a long account of my movements, even if the final line was added at a later date, it will also be noted that although I had said one had left me opposite the church, I was referring to the youngest boy, the other left behind the O.T. building.

Let me explain the O.T. [Occupational Therapy] Building, it is about 50-60 feet long, the boys were playing in the bushes at the far end from the church, one boy went back within a few yards, the other followed me as far as the road, where I told him to return to his friends.

It also should be noted, that from where the children's den was, which was to one side of the hospital and not in front of it, it was only possible to see about a third of the church. Oh I went back a week before writing this chapter, to seek more information, but it was impossible to say where anyone was going, once they reached the end of the path.

R:30 is straightforward and so is R:32 but wait a moment, here I had told the police about the little girls playing on the heap of sand, then in Q: 36. The police asked me if I know the heap of sand the girls were playing on, Hold It! Wasn't it my brain that was supposed to be dozy?

In R:37. Is an obvious sign of being observant and the compost heap was probably the one I had taken them to the previous night, not the main one on the plans, which I was to discover existed, when I went back to the Lord Chancellors Office, for all intents and purposes such a fact of taking them to it, was conveniently "overlooked?" by the police.

Okay it could be argued, that if that was the case, why did the police exclaim I hadn't told them about it the night before, yet made no comment on the implied situation, I had not told them about the girls, filling in the holes behind the church or going to the farm after leaving the girls.

In R: 51. I obviously knew where to look for eggs…I had worked on a dairy and poultry farm, even if it had been a year earlier, but for a psychopath or schizophrenic I had a very retentive memory.

R:52 was straightforward and R:55 was almost a repeated word for word statement as it appears in Launder's statement, between No.18 and No.19 made on the

Saturday about midnight, after going through a lot of questioning and a medical examination, plus having been up since 7 a.m., now two days later I recount the discussion I had "Had" with the children about arranging to meet the next day to make bows and arrows, No mention of making them that night.

One boy obviously misunderstood and was followed by the youngest boy, when I explained the situation to the eldest boy, he returned to his friends, whilst the youngest walked on as far as the road.

R:58. May sound a bit vague, but I still rarely take note of important numbers until I need to know them, then usually write them down on a piece of paper, the only numbers I know by heart, is my front door number, date of birth and N.I. number [I am slightly dyslexic with numbers], which just about covers everyone who reads this book, so we have a lot more in common, even if you have never had a weak bladder.

R: 67. I was fairly well informed about the laws, governing animal welfare, which I had probably been told to me a few days earlier, when I went there with some farm workers.

R: 74. I obviously had no idea where the blood had come from, but probably when wiping it off, noticed all the straw on my shoe and took it for granted it was off the compost heap, having just climbed up one in the hope of finding an egg.

R: 76. Well it still makes sense to use a dark coloured hanky, even in this statement by me, I gave a fairly obvious account of why I preferred a coarse hanky to a fine one…then more inventions come along.

R: 80. Okay I nicked a length of cord off the curtains, [not exactly a kleptomaniac], when I returned to the ward, it was still in my pocket, when the police took my clothing away, note it was also referred to by Dr Cliff's statement Exhibit 37, referring to the string in my pocket, which must have been taken as I entered the ward, because it had not occurred to me; "That I may have some in my locker". R.81.

Now to go back to the statement as a whole subject.

The next part of his statement I am going to be pointing out, as it took me quite some time to discover how and where it was done, those strange little comments or digressions from the situation in hand, okay I digress myself, but at least the digressions are usually; directly relating to what I am talking about, even if at first it is obvious, but these seem to imply I was more than merely naïve, but as we have already seen between Q: 35. Q: 36 and Q: 37 and note in R: 32 I had just told them about talking to the girls playing on the sand heap.

Then they asked me if I knew of the sand heap, I had just referred to and then asked, if I was talking to them, we were having a conversation about a cat, of course I spoke to them, do you see what I mean; that this statement has been glorified, don't forget it was a hand written statement, later to be typed, during which slightly more impressive things can be added, only they were not all that clever about the insertions, but then who would be reading it with a questioning mind, there is obviously no chance of the accused ever getting his hands on the statement…!

As I have already said several times, maybe I will never be allowed to clear my name, but if I can prevent what has happened to me, happening to someone else, regardless to whether or not they have weak bladders, then the very fact I have tried, may in another small way; to Justify the writing of this book.

I will explain later a small law, which with all the evidence I have discovered; I am still not allowed to take it to court [even my friendly High Court Barrister, had never previously heard of it, but its somewhere in a very obscure law book], oh I will cover it now, it appears that because all the questions I am asking now, My Q.C. should have asked at the time of the trial, but as he did not, it now appears that, if I had not been satisfied with my Q.C. I had every Right under the Law, to write a letter to the judge, point out my complaints and then request another Q.C.!

So it's My Own Fault I was convicted for the crime, on the grounds that in every library, there is a book in which it is stated very clearly, but the fact I never read books at that time or was told the book existed, or what to look up, regardless of the fact it took me 36 years to discover the law existed, [even though I have still not found it]!

Is no defence to a Judge, who will say that; Ignorance of the Law is No Defence in a Court of British Justice, with only a very small minority of those wearing the wigs, aware of such a law…

Note it takes 7 years of intensive study to get on the first step of becoming a Judge, why 7 years, when Joe Blogs', only has to walk into a library and become an expert in Law or should that read; "Anyone who cannot accept the postulations of British Justice are not Paedophiles!" Considering just how many paedophiles are given absolute protection by the law and the police, even those in prison are given special protection and are always discharged after serving a third of their sentence, whereas everyone else has to have served at least half of their sentence before being considered for parole.

Don't forget; "The Laws of the Land, are only to Protect the Law Makers and Judges, Not the Public!"

Now I appreciate clever questioning, requires throwing in some otherwise unrelated things on the spur of the moment, to catch a person off guard, in the hope they may slip up.

But look at section R: 75 to R: 79; I had already taken them to the bucket in which I had put my hanky; on the Saturday Night, so why ask about the colour.

This was part of the subject of Saturday night when I had taken my shoes off. Re; Launder's statement No.11; "I then pointed out the wet matter on his left shoe and asked what it was. He said: It's some stuff off the compost heap."

But to return to Launder's statement;

At which point it should have been obvious I was talking about the hanky, having wiped my shoe with it and placing it in a bucket of water.

That was before taking them to the Farm Office to show them the hanky in a bucket, which he claims he saw in a dark barn, No. 25; "Whilst in the barn I saw a bucket containing what looked like blood stained water and a blood stained handkerchief; the hanky is Exhibit 21. It was found in building "R" on the plan…the Farm Office.

Yes I agree, this would have been an intelligent thing for an average teenager to do, but I had suffered all my life with incontinence, hence after wetting my bed, I was made to soak my sheets in a bucket of cold water to dilute the stains, before being punished and then washing them. I was hardly going to put a hanky covered in blood and straw, back into my pocket.

When I returned to Garlands Hospital recently, most of the farm had been demolished, but the barn "Q" and the office "R" are boarded up, but I made a strange discovery; if we had been in the barn looking for a sack, it would have been impossible to see the bucket from the barn itself.

A slight but hopefully you will agree interesting digression, when I first started to copy these statements, I thought both would prove; I wasn't trying to hide anything, because the obvious lies were so easy to see in the first statement, but as the second statement wasn't signed by anyone, it could be seen as neither here nor there.

But going through the second statement carefully and referring back to Launder's statement thinking; well Launder said one thing two days earlier, that would disprove some of the accusations and implications in the second.

Yet just prior to No.31. There is this paragraph: "At about 3 p.m. on 6th March 1961, with D/Supt Oldcorn, I saw the accused in the presence of his solicitor. The accused was questioned and he replied to "My" questions."

Is it any wonder that the second statement was not signed by anyone? They were both written by the same person!

Don't forget, he points out that all my clothing, was given to him and he had handed over to forensics', which seems to add a few queries to the validity of his two statements?

Which may help everyone, especially myself start to realize why the first statement made little sense and the second statement, almost no sense at all, in the way it's been written out, but I think I should add here, that although the language and paragraphs may have read a little strange, that I created the paragraphs, but I created the paragraphs, to make each point understandable, the original statement was five and a half pages long, but written out as one continuous paragraph or five and a half paragraphs.

Which I suppose could make life easier for most people, but I have found that when life seems to be going easy for me, it gets very complicated.

So the strange discoveries I keep coming across, are whilst I am writing this, it's probably because I am asking a second person to refer backwards, as something odd comes into my mind, that I am made more aware of the strangeness of each statements.

All the days and dates and times in Launder's original statement flow continuously from the end of one sentence into the next. It should also be noted that the first statement ended with experiments, he made in the drain system of the slaughterhouse, that took place on 14th of March 1961, but the second statement was written and typed on the 6th of March 1961.

Now am I being just slightly paranoid or does it strike You also; as being slightly strange, the second statement was not only referred to in the first statement, but written by the same person!

Yes I know a lot of people will be asking the same question, about why didn't my Q.C. spot any of these things, after all he must have had copies of both statements, as well as the statements of the children and other witnesses, plus a plan of the farm.

In the beginning of the book, I said that my Q.C. didn't seem interested in my case and refused to point out things I had asked him to. Well if we have a preview of part of the next chapter, which will

be covering the Press items of the trial, not that the Press can be relied on for exact reports, it will put a few people at ease, if the above sounds too farfetched, but if I copy out now; My Defence Q.C's opening statement to the Court, it will quickly be seen; he was of the same opinion of the police and everyone else involved, that as I was in a mental hospital it was an open and shut case, that I was a lunatic and not just an institutionalised naïve kid.

Cumberland News. 19.5.61. Front Page. [Before I was to give evidence]. "Mr Burrell opening the case for the defence said that there were two main questions: Who murdered the little boy and the state of Peck's mind?"

It adds later: "The defence evidence that would be called would be that he is suffering from a psychopathic disorder."

Well with a Friend like that, who needs enemies?

But then maybe that is what British Justice relies upon…The Prosecution, The Police and the Defence; All being on the same side, for after all, "Great Minds Think Alike" or could it be a case of; "Anyone in a nut house must be insane, otherwise why would they be in there?!"

Here's me thinking; that during my return to society, as my life seemed so complicated, I just fitted in where I could and wandered along as best as I could, but obviously my life became complicated even before I left the Homes, what with people making strange statements during observations of extremely highly trained child psychologist, that a kid must have been using a higher level of psychology against…go back to the opening of the Social Reports:

"28/9/58. I found no evidence of emotional disturbance, which is strange when his case history is considered."

The Fates must have had a really sick sense of humour, the day that I was born by giving me the gift of mirth, which must have been all those years ago, bordering onto the cynical, think back to my early life, whenever I was known to be in any form of pain, physical or emotional to the extent I cried, I was always punished!

Even when being beaten with a cane, I was not allowed to cry, well I was; if I wanted extra strokes, for crying like a baby, when I was 5 years old!

So it should stand to reason, that by the time I was 14 years old, I needed to be interviewed by a Human Being, not some weirdo with an impressive array of postulations that implied; the psychotic pervert was in any position of Authority, he added late; "I appear to have no deep affection for anyone" obviously referring to adults!

Yet again I seem to have digressed a little too far, off the topic of the second statement.

So back to the second statement, even if I lament, there wasn't a copy of My Own Statement, in the files at the Lord Chancellors Office, in fact I wonder if the Home Office has one still, because it must conflict very strongly against these two statements that have been allowed to remain on the files.

I was covering the Odd Statements within the statement; Q.1. has already been covered, well the last line in it.

Q5. "You said that you left him at half past four at the corner of the laundry is that right?"

Well considering I had told him about the girls playing in the sand, after going behind the church to fill in some holes, having left the boys a 4.15 p.m., even if they had persuaded someone [probably himself] to suggest I was with the girls before the bus left.

This leaves an even bigger question mark over where the laundry came into it, even if it can't be mistaken for O.T. even if I had mumbled it.

10R. I think I have already covered, having already stated in his other statement, just prior to No.13, how blood got onto my trousers. Then in this one I apparently claimed: "I don't remember seeing it there!"

In R11 I said I went to the farm with three or four boys, but halfway through describing the boys in R13, having described two, I stopped and said; a nurse had arrived in his car, which with that line and down to R18 would make more sense if it came after R22. Except even within those lines in Q17 he asked; if that had been the last time I went into the farm yard, already aware I had gone looking for eggs after speaking to the girls.

R13. Also will cause a few questions in your minds; when you read the newspaper reports. Because I apparently described one of the boys as being "The Farmers Son" well how on earth was I to have known that fact, which you will discover later was not a fact at all, because during the time I was at the farm, the farmer was half a mile away, observing his son playing near the hospital power station, with a man wearing the clothing of a hospital patient, whilst at that time I was wearing school clothing.

Maybe the claim I was playing with the farmer's son, was to either imply; I was yet again, in two places at the same time, which even if I had been a schizophrenic, would have still been a physical impossibility or were they implying that the farmer being a yokel, did not recognise his own son, from a distance of less than 50 feet.

I am sure the line in Q24 was an accidental oversight during Launder's eagerness to trip me up; as he rearranged these statements, he made a right mess of it when he stated; "You told us, you remember the other night that you went back to the farm for another purpose."

I had told him about going to look for eggs, after leaving the girls, two days previously, he later erased it from his first statement, but needed me to deny going back to the farm, so inadvertently whilst referring to his other notes, borrowed the wrong answer to use as a question.

R27. Last two lines, we already have Philomena's statement; saying that after I left her, I went in the direction of the farm, yet here as in a few other places, I apparently went straight from the O.T. to the laundry, let's put it this way, if you were stood where the boys were playing, looking straight ahead, the church door would be at 12 o'clock and the laundry at 2 o'clock, as the crow flies, but

you would have had to walk pass the corner of the O.T. then turn right for a couple of hundred yards, to reach the corner of the laundry, whereas the church was at 11 o'clock.

R28. After having gone in for my tea, making a point of washing my hands [old childhood habits die hard] before sitting down at the table, but apparently because I saw the football coming on, I decided to watch it, instead of having my tea, that I had returned to the ward for, I wasn't on medication, so I could have stayed out until 9 p.m., if I hadn't been hungry, because even in those days I wasn't a television potato, I just watched it if something interesting was on.

So this means we should narrow the times down a bit, because it was after having my tea, did I approach the TV and saw the tele-type, Q29. So the only way I could have known about it, was to have seen it on the screen.

In Q31 He states: "We have been told etc." What medication was he on, he obviously had a terrible memory for a detective, as I had told him I had met the German, who could confirm I was on my own, the fact he was never called to court, is probably exactly what he did tell them, plus I wasn't walking towards the laundry.

Q35. Seems to imply; the girls had told him, that after I had been speaking to them; I had gone to the farm with the little boy.

Q36 and Q37 must speak for themselves, that this was a further error added later, having told him in R32 I had been talking to them on the sand heap.

R40, Q41 and R41, the odd memory about the little red shovel, especially after apparently given a perfectly detailed description about what each boy had been carrying in the first statement No. 4/5., with dimensions to the stick, then the next question is; "When did he have that with him?" Reply: "I think he had it with him all the afternoon." Yet I had spent 3 hours with my visitor during the afternoon.

There seem to be a few statements implying; I had been playing with them the whole afternoon, that were never queried in court, but then my visitor who would have been an important witness, was never asked to make a statement, nor attend the court as a witness .

Q44. After apparently saying I had left him at the laundry, I am asked; "And did you see him again after the First time I left him at the laundry?"

The "First Time?" How many times was I supposed to have taken him to the laundry, you will discover later how Launder wanted to prove to the court, that after leaving the girls and going to the farm, he implied; I returned to where the boys were playing and took the boy to the farm, which made it so important; to have spoken to the girls 25 minutes before I stopped to speak to them, but he had failed to read Philomena's statement, because when she returned to where the little boys were playing, the little boy wasn't with them.

I still feel that whoever took him to the farm, must have been well known to the child and probably would not have been noticed as out of the ordinary, on the other hand, If I had taken him towards the laundry or the farm, had my visitor left earlier than 4 p.m. at least a dozen or more people, would have noticed us, as it would have been unusual to see me walking around with a solitary child.

Q46. "Did you yourself go into the farm after you spoke to the girls?"

R46. "No" then the subject seems to again until Q52"How long did you stay talking to the little girls." Shouldn't this come before or immediately after Q46?

Q63. Edmond Castle hanky with 42 on it, to which I replied: R63 about my button being found in the pig sty, why would anyone ask that as a reply to the hanky question…yet no more is said about the hanky until Q75, now either Q63 or Q75 are pure invention.

Also in this statement; reference is only made to one hanky being found, yet later it becomes two hankies being found and marked in biro with the numbers of the two boys, who had been at the hospital over a 15 month period, which sounds just too much of a convenient coincidence, that I should have accidentally been issued with a second hanky, that had been the number of another boy who had been to the hospital.

I wonder who discovered that the other boy had been to the hospital and exactly what his number had been, I am not implying, but on the Sunday morning the Police did visit the school to get a couple of hankies which Dr Cliff compared only the material of them.

No Perish the Thought, for after all we have discovered in D/C Launder's two statements…it's unthinkable…in England…a bent copper…England is Not a Police State…IS IT…They only exist in Fascist Regimes!

Maybe those at the Home Office didn't compare both statements; otherwise the unsigned one would have vanished, along with other evidence.

The above may explain, why he needed to dump the case on any easy to frame victim…maybe he was related to the murderer …Surely the blood on the toe of my sock, would have stood out like a lighthouse , considering there was so much blood to still be wet the next morning when examined, then He observed a scratch on the back of my finger, yet the doctor who took nail clippings from myself stated: He saw no blood or injury to any part of my body, except a scab that may not have bled for some time, so who else apart from Launder saw; "This Scratch on My Finger?" Which implied a great deal considering that; "Just by Coincidence" the child had blood and sand under one of his finger nails?

Let's chat about a "Fortunate Coincidence" that Launder discovered and used to his advantage, was when as he took my shoes from me [which is a moot point… do the police take preference over doctors, when it comes to undressing and examining a suspect] I pointed out the blood on them, he had just discovered the child was dead and here was I a local Looney with blood on my shoes, maybe it was at this moment in time he decided that as I knew I had blood on them, end of reality and the beginning of a perfect frame up.

Maybe he put the left shoe and left sock into the same bag, then that would explain why all the blood, sand and chaff, as well as the straw, disappeared from the outside of my shoe and the animal blood became human blood that became absorbed into my plastic shoe and drained to the toe of the sock, but what happened to the straw etcetera?

*   *   *   *   *

Although as earlier in the book, I know I was encourage to say something or other in the witness box that was meant to help find me guilty [which failed], but I had been convinced to say I hadn't returned to the farm, after speaking to the girls or did I deny returning to the farm "twice" after meeting the girls, but sadly we do not have the questions recorded during the trial…more evidence destroyed after the trial or was that because I had been found guilty of the crime,[well it was claimed, I was found guilty under circumstantial evidence, that could not prove I was guilty, but I had not produced enough evidence to say I wasn't guilty, but still locked away to protect the public from a dangerous psychopath.

But having said that, why was just enough evidence retained for historical purposes that were never meant to see the light of day, until everyone involved had died?

*   *   *   *   *

Chapter 5

Myself and my brother a few months before being arrested and mistaken for a man.

Newspaper Reports.

This chapter covers the newspaper reports, mainly in the Cumberland News and the Cumberland Evening News.

I agree that the Press is not the most reliable organ, when it comes to exact reproduction, but it will give you an idea of what was reported, under the circumstances of "An Open and Shut Case".

Plus you will all have a clearer idea of what the jury were unaware of, such as the original statements and forensic evidence from three medical experts.

Also I will only copy the main statements, not the trivia leading up to them, let me put it this way: "The trial of Malcolm John William Peck, a 17 year old, mental hospital patient," and just the initials and not the first names etcetera, if constantly repeated.

We already know this is the trial that is being reported.

But I will quote the dates, if anyone finds these quotes just a little too farfetched, they can go to the Central Library in Carlisle, it is located in; "The Lanes" in Scotch Street or at the British Museum Library, with an advantage over myself, i.e. You will have the names of the papers, dates and page numbers, without having to wait a further 3 hours, if you ask for the wrong papers.

First I will try to fill in some information collected on 17.1.96. Then after reading a lot of quotes in the library, I returned to the hospital, to take "strolling" times.

Most of the farm has been demolished [maybe due to the motorway that was built over much of the land], but the buildings "Q" and "R" still exist, even though boarded up, the farm entrance has gone, along with the slaughterhouse and other buildings.

I met a few patients who were there at the time, but they have spent so much time on medication, it has become a vague memory, I also asked when tea time is, they all vouched it was still at 4.30 p.m. and has been for as long as they can remember, it may seem a trivial point, but confused people need some sort of routine, so meal times never change, as I had my tea before watching the football results coming on, had me in the ward at between 4.25 p.m. to 4.30 p.m.

Then I retraced the journey I had made, [a slight digression, when I was a sighted guide for the blind, we went for long walks, but some of the guys wanted to walk faster, so I took them on ahead of the main party, but was told to take another volunteer with me, who was in the SAS and had a map, when we reached some white gates, I led them single file onto the road, then saw some other white gates and I apologised, for joining the road too early, then the SAS Officer, asked if I lived in the area, to which I replied; No, but we came this way, last year, oh it was about 5 miles, through woods and heathland before reaching the road, then was told she wished some of her trainees could be taught so quickly how to use landmarks, it doesn't really matter where I go, the second time is always easier] although some of the buildings and farm fences had been removed and a few added, but as I had waited maybe; 5 minutes that may have seemed like 10, to see the matron of the female ward, spoke to the boys for a minute or two, filled in some holes, spoke to the girls, looked for some eggs, washed my hands etcetera, I added ten minutes to my renewed journey, I also did the journey a second time, which was not a very casual stroll, owing to "Keep Out" signs and looking nothing like a patient or employee.

The second journey took 17 minutes to walk, adding a conservative 10 minutes, making it 27 minutes; from the bus leaving to entering the ward.

I walked the length of the "Then O.T. Building", which is now the; Staff Social Club, a distance of 44 normal paces or say 60 feet in length, all the bushes have been removed, but it is impossible to see more than a third of the church, so at that time, only a few feet of the church would have been visible, due to overhanging evergreen branches.

I suppose it goes without saying; that each item will be followed by an observation of my own, i.e. *1 *2 etcetera.

Another point to take into consideration is that you have a better idea of what was being said than the jury, who had no statements to refer to, made by the witnesses within hours or days of the murder.

Oh yes one other point, because a lot of the press reports are long drawn out affairs, in fact two thirds of the report on 21.4.61. is an exact reproduction of the report in the same paper the day before. 20.4.61.

Therefore except in some "strange" instances, I will only be quoting quotes of statements, made by the witnesses, including police observations.

Source of Reference; Cumberland Evening News, Monday March 6th. 1961. Front Page Story.

Policemen in the hunt for the killer of a four year old boy who was found battered to death in the grounds of Garlands Mental Hospital, near Carlisle, have made no further progress, it was reported today.

Meanwhile as the investigation goes on, an inquest is being arranged by the County Coroner's Office for late this afternoon or early this evening.

The body of little George Warwick, the son of a farm worker on the home farm at the hospital, was found lying in a small enclosed yard at the rear of the farm on Saturday night.

His head was battered and the body had been pushed under rusting metal sheets. *1.

George, who lived only 500 yards away at Fell View on the Garlands Estate, was missed at 5.30 p.m. and his alarmed parents, 30 year old Mr David Warwick and his wife Elizabeth, aged 27, reported his disappearance to the police at 7.15 p.m.

A search party, made up of about 30 estate workers and policemen, was organised immediately and one of the workers found the body.

Officers of the Cumberland and Westmorland Police, led by D/Supt Thomas Oldcorn, of the CID at Penrith Headquarters and Supt Neil Milne, in charge of Carlisle County Division, spent all day yesterday at the farm, they were there again early this morning.

A two hour post mortem examination was conducted at the Cumberland Infirmary by Dr Colin Corby, a Home Office pathologist, from Newcastle Forensic Science Laboratory and Dr J S Faulds, chief pathologist at the Infirmary.

After it, Supt Milne said that the death had been due to head injuries.

Supt Oldcorn said: "We are treating this as a murder case. Our enquiries are being confined to the hospital."

During the investigation at the farm, Mr John Murphy, a male nurse who lives near the Warwicks, brought three of his children to the yard to help the police.

They were playing tag and cowboys and Indians with the dead boy on the day he died, the children walked hand in hand with policemen in and around the farm buildings, pointing out where they had played.

Police found a toy double barrelled shotgun belonging to George in a barn and took it away for examination. *2.

George was the second of a family of four children. His father is understood to have seen him talking to a man in the clothes of a mental patient. *3.

The hospital has almost 1000 patients and certain types of patient can stroll around the grounds.

The scene of the death is only about half a mile away from the large Carlisle suburb of Harraby, and parents there are keeping a close watch on their children. Unquote.

I copied out the whole for several reasons, some of which you may have already noticed, during the reading of it; Okay some of it may have been invented by the press or various people reported what they knew also, *1. The body was pushed under rusting iron sheets, there is no mention to these in any police statement or in the photos of the yard, and there were no sheets of iron.

*2. "The police found a double barrelled shotgun, belonging to the boy in a barn and took it away." In the statement he had a stick all the afternoon.

*3. The father seeing his son talking to a man in the clothes of a hospital patient, I will cover that later, as it is an important piece of information [oh I think I have covered that already, because at the time he saw his son and the patient, I was on the other side of the hospital, wearing school clothing and at 16, I could not be mistaken as a man, by a 30 year old man…see the photographs].

*   *   *   *   *

Cumberland News. Friday March 10th. Page 5, [second appearance in court].

A sixteen year old youth who was accused on Tuesday of the murder of George Taylor Warwick…will make his second appearance before Cumberland Ward Juvenile Court next Tuesday.

He was arrested at 6.30 p.m. on Monday---48 hours after the body of the little boy…was found in a yard at the rear of the hospital farm.

D/Sgt Albert Launder of the County Police said he arrested the youth and took him to Police Headquarters in Abbey Street. The youth was cautioned and accused and he replied: "I didn't."

The Chairman, Miss Mary Chance, told the youth: "You will be remanded in custody to Durham Prison until then. The bench thinks you are too unruly a character to go to a remand home.

George was found under some iron sheets [*4] after his parents reported him missing.

For nearly two days, officers of the Cumberland and Westmorland Police under Supt. Thomas Oldcorn of the C.I.D. Penrith and Supt. Neil Milne of Carlisle County Division made enquiries at the hospital. Unquote.

*4 again those iron sheets appeared. The comment of Miss Chance could be that any 16 year old youth, charged with any kind of murder, would be remanded automatically in prison.

*   *   *   *   *

This next statement is a merely cynical insert, because what happened prior to it was I had appeared before the juvenile court on my 17th Birthday.
Cumberland News. Friday March 24th. 1961. P.13.
"…He has previously made two brief appearances at the Cumberland Ward Juvenile Court, but last Friday, March 17th, he became 17, and on Tuesday he came before the adult court.
This means his identity can now be given; He is Malcolm John William Peck, c/o Garlands Hospital. Unquote.

*   *   *   *   *

These next two are fairly long; they are the hearing before the main trial.
Cumberland News. Thurs. April 20th. 1961. Pages 1 & 11.
"A Jigsaw of circumstantial and scientific evidence showed clearly how four year old George Taylor Warwick, of Fell View, Harraby, Carlisle, was murdered said Mr John Wood, appearing for the Director of Public Prosecutions, at the county Magistrates Court today.

The various pieces by themselves might not appear to say much, but when put together one gets a very clear picture, he said.

Mr Wood alleged that the picture "points overwhelmingly" to M.J.W.Peck, a 17 year old schoolboy accused of the killing.

Peck whose address was given as c/o Garlands Mental Hospital, Carlisle has denied throughout that he was responsible for the little boy's death, he added.

When Mr Wood opened the case for the prosecution, he said that George Warwick lived very close to the hospital.

During a full scale search that followed, Mr J Briggs found George's body. It was lying in the Western corner of a pen in the yard of the hospitals farm, near the doors of the slaughterhouse.

The boy's body was in a large pool of blood, his hands were tied behind his back and his trousers were below his knees. From stains on the boy and his clothing, it appeared some sort of indecency had taken place.

A post mortem examination showed bruises and cuts on the head, face and legs.*1. The skull was fractured on the left side under a bleeding wound. The cause of death was given as cerebral haemorrhage and a fractured skull. *2.

Mr Wood alleged that there is "a wealth of circumstantial and scientific evidence against Peck, he told how a trouser button, a button thread, a jacket fibre, two handkerchiefs, blood and other stains had been discovered and analysed. There was also evidence about a football match result.

He gave the prosecutions account of Peck's movements just before and after the boy died. On the afternoon it happened, Peck was seen in the farm yard with some young boys including George.*3.

At 4.10 p.m. he was seen talking to three girls at a sand heap, near where the body was found. *4.

Between then and 4.30. he returned to where the young children were and asked them if they wanted to make a bow and arrow. *5

Peck and the murdered boy were seen walking together near where the body was later found, alleged Mr Wood. The accused was next seen in a ward at the hospital at 4.45 p.m.*6

When he was questioned, Peck said he had left the "little ginger haired boy" at the corner of the laundry and went in for his tea.

On that day Peck was anxious to know the result of a football match between Southend and Bristol City, and he had told the doctor about it. The result was flashed on the television screen at 4.41. but when a doctor asked Peck what the result had been he gave the wrong answer. *7

One would have thought that he would have remembered whether his team had won or lost, said Mr Wood. This would probably help the magistrate to decide whether or not Peck was in his ward when he said he was.

Bloodstains were found on the left leg of Peck's trousers. When questioned about them he said they had got there when he was giving blood.

This was checked and it was found that he had a faulty injection, but when it happened the blood had seemed to fall on his right trouser leg, said Mr Wood. *8

Blood was also found in the crevices in the pattern on the toes of the accused shoes. The absence of blood from the upper surface of the toe seemed to indicate that it had been wiped. *9

There was also blood on the side of the shoe. When this was examined the day after the little boy's death, it was still wet. *10

When questioned about this, Peck had said that he wiped his shoes on some sacking which had meat and slaughterhouse refuse on it from the farm compost heap. *11.

But when the compost heap was examined the next day it was quite dry and firm. Peck took officers to a barn to find the sacking but could not do so. *12.

At this point is an insert: "Her Cat failed to get In. Before the start of the hearing a woman entered the court with a cat, wearing a collar and a lead, beneath her coat. She was told the animal was not allowed in the room." *13

He left the school before the laundry came and it was the custom for the staff to give you some clothing from a number not in use if you were short, the prosecution said. *14.

[I will go onto direct evidence of witnesses.]

Evidence that he saw Peck with the boy a 1.15 p.m. on March 4 was given by John Paton. *15

Peck was seen again at 3.50 p.m. by Marjorie Warwick, ward sister, who said accused handed her a parcel and left. *16

He was again seen between 3.50 and 4 p.m. by Mr William Johnson, a farm labourer.*17

A male nurse in Peck's ward Mr Thomas Ellwood, said he did not see the accused at 4.30, but did see him between 4.45 and 4.50 p.m. sitting in front of the television.

I don't think Malcolm Peck was watching television when the sports results came on said Ronald Steele, aged 20, a patient at Garlands Hospital.

Mr Steele told the magistrate he first saw Peck about 5 p.m. when he noticed him watching television. *18

Four school children, three boys and a girl gave evidence that they saw the accused a number of times on the afternoon of March 4th.

*1. When did those bruises appear on his legs? Because there was no mention of them in the forensic reports.

*2. From Ailsa Thomson, Legal Officer of; "Justice" quote; "I see in addition that the boy died from a fractured skull...In these circumstances blood staining on clothes is unusual in my experience, because the surface of the skull is rarely smashed up and the blood tends to flow from the ears, nose or mouth consequent upon the damage to the brain. In other words, it flows out following the injury rather than spurting on impact." unquote

*3. This is one of those clever comments from Launder's statement, when I stated I was playing with 3 boys at midday in the farm, one of them became the farmer's son, suggesting that I knew who the boy was and presumably having been playing with him at lunch time, the boy would not have had seconds thoughts about returning with me a second time to the farm, but as you

read further, You will discover that; not only was this boy not the farmer's son, but the farmer saw his son talking to a man wearing patients clothing half a mile away, at precisely the same time, as the police claim; I claimed I was playing with his son in the farm yard.

*4. Now this is interesting, as they were only using an estimate to the time the child died, how could they suggest what my movements were after the boy died, there is no mention of what they had been in this report.

*5. Then I was seen talking to the girls at 4.10 p.m. now we already know in the original statement of William Johnson, who saw me talking to the girls, that he had claimed saw me at 3.50 p.m. and was not in the farm between 4.10 to 4.50 p.m. okay it was a contrived statement, considering the bus my visitor left on did not leave until 4 o'clock…which had been confirmed.

[This is going to sound a bit cynical, but although it can be said the sand heap, was close to where the girls were playing…the way the crow flies…it was a few hundred yards to the farm gate, then maybe 30 yards north of the gate, before going back in line to where the girls were playing, but this statement implies, it was very close to where the girls were playing…it's like saying Southend is 7 miles from the Isle of Grain…but by road it must be at least 50 to 60 miles, but it would not be dishonest to say it was 7 miles…unless using the measure for dishonest reasons.]

*6. What a clever suggestion, that after going to the farm, I returned to where the children were playing, but I was observed by Philomena heading towards the farm, as she returned to where the children were and George wasn't with them, so it was a physical impossibility to return and then take the boy away… a point carefully avoided in the court, plus the fact that the police made absolutely no effort to discover who the person was wearing patients clothing, as seen by the farmer and who knows how many more people …All the afternoon when I was with my visitor.

The bow and arrow idea was put to the boys for the next day's events; "Before" I started the journey to fill in the holes behind the church and meeting the girls playing in the sand.

Also the police tried to imply I had doubled back after meeting the girls and then took the boy to the farm, I had timed my journey, when I returned recently to the hospital, it took 17 minutes without stopping to talk to anyone, then added another 10 minutes for the stopping to chat to the girls and double back, so this would have been an impossible feat, as when the girls had walked in the opposite direction towards the boys, the boy was not with them, which means if I had doubled back, I would have had to search the hospital grounds to find him.

*7. Anyone would think I had a heavy bet on the match, that I was unaware was taking place. Maybe I should give this its own chapter and call it A Football Joke that Backfired! Which in reality is exactly what happened, in fact I did not say they had won or lost, I just said they always win, although it was repeated throughout the case, no one checked to see if Southend was at the Top of the league table…in fact I still couldn't tell you of one particular score by them, this was said before the boy's body was found and I didn't realise the seriousness of the reply, I had just been bantering, so I told just the one little white lie, as a silly brag. Okay there was that weird statement by the supreme being, in charge of the hospital, who claimed to have interviewed me and all my answers were completely different, except mumbling a score I was already aware of, plus there is not one signed statement by him, in any of the files, think about it, he was apparently my doctor, but no statements about any apparent interviews with me, throughout the time I was there or by any other doctor.

*8. Blood was found on my left trouser leg, plus I happen to be right handed, although I don't have many injections or blood test. It has always been taken from my left arm or injections put into my left arm or buttock, I have no idea why this is so, but if blood falls from the needle in my left arm it is hardly going to fall on my right trouser leg, unless I was sitting casually with crossed legs, but I have a bit of a phobia about injection needles and have never received one casually, which is a good thing I suppose, as I may have started Main-lining years ago and became a Big H Addict!

*9. I don't understand this statement, as it seems to imply the child was kicked to death, but there is no reference to this, as the pattern on the shoe, was not on the toe, but midway between the top of the toe and the front of the ankle.

*10. Well that is interesting, where did this blood on the "side" of the shoe come from, regardless of it still being wet the next day…maybe the reporter was slightly deaf and misheard "Inside" but then did the jury also mishear this as well or was it twisted by the prosecution and my court elected Q.C., that there was Wet Blood on: "The side of the shoe" that had been overlooked by the two forensic scientist!

*11. But where did the sack covered in meat and slaughterhouse refuge come from, a rather convenient discovery after Launder invented the sack, [Re: No.21 in statement], but who decided the meat wasn't wiped off but onto the shoe?

*12. It doesn't say whether or not they walked over the compost heap, i.e. the surface of farm slurry or the mud in a drying pond, can be very dry on the surface until walked on, when a person's weight causes them to sink, note I only had it on one shoe, which should indicate I started to climb the heap, placing all my weight on the one foot that then sank, even if it take a little while to notice the mess on them…how long does it take a person to realise they have stood in dog-shit, before walking it onto their carpets at home.

*13. I know I mentioned her being in court, but Why wasn't she called as a witness, considering I had been with her the whole afternoon, plus the girls must have said something, considering they had been playing with her cat in the afternoon, during which several people had observed a man wearing patients clothing, talking to the boy, most of the time I was with her, but then they did not call any of my other witnesses, referred to in my statement… [Was the patient known to them, did he have influential parents, that blinded the police to reality or should that be bribed to look the other way] or would it have embarrassed the Prosecution and my Defence, if I had several witnesses that could vouch for my whereabouts during those crucial times, I needed to be somewhere else, let alone how embarrassing for the jury to discover how evil and corrupt British Justice really is., if my Defence [?] had produced factual evidence as opposed to circumstantial evidence or could it be called postulations of logic?

*14. My number was 42, but number 30 had once been used by

an S Smith, who had been to the hospital, but at the time I was there, it was reallocated to Greene who had never been to Garlands... note Only Numbers "Not in Use" were given to other boys, therefore I wasn't given his hanky, I still remember Greene, he was a tiny weak boy, who wanted to become a Fire Man in the Fire Brigade and we were close friends, plus the school did its own laundry.

*15. Evidence that a man wearing patients clothing, was seen talking to some children at 1.15 p.m. was given by John Paton, but Mr Warwick [the child's father] observed the other person speaking to his son.500 yards away, at precisely the same time!

*16. A small open trifle can hardly be mistaken for a parcel and we already know the bus left at 4 p.m., plus she claimed I delivered it 10 minutes before the bus left...coercion?

*17. This is interesting as he is the person who saw me talking to the girls and had already pointed out seeing me at 4.10 p.m.

*18. Pardon? What sort of statement is that, he doesn't think I was watching the results and the first time he saw me was at 5 p.m. I was sat next to him, so maybe he was asleep, because the nurse saw me watching it 10-15 minutes before the guy sitting next to me did, but then in R.30 it seems there must have been several witnesses sitting there, because one complained I had nicked his seat or could it be he was the only witness willing to twist the facts to help the police.

Before going into the next report, there are a couple of observations, worth mentioning [if you haven't already questioned them yourselves.

1. Why were they constantly harping on about a scar on my ankle, that had healed before going to the hospital, rather than sticking to the facts, they choose to ignore.

2. How many times is the fact I was in a mental hospital, followed by the number of suggestions I was a psychopath...or could this be to brain wash the jury, that it will be their fault, if they find me not guilty and a very dangerous psychopath is released into society, due to their incompetence, being fully aware that I suffered with severe incontinence...and everyone knows they will become schizophrenics.

3. Apart from hitting a freak who was raping me in my sleep, just what other evidence is there, that I was/am a very dangerously violent person, with a long history of attacking children and adults, none that I can discover, prior to the case or on eventual discharge into society…okay I did use a tongue in cheek threat, to the GP to see a urologist…which is hardly an act of treason… yet!

But then it did upset a lot of GP's and other nonce cases, that love to promote violence and sexual abuse of children, by proving it is possible for the bladder [just like any other organ in the body] to fail to disconnect at birth and function naturally.

I know it sounds as if I am being cynical at times, but it is not in mirth, even if sometimes mirth does creep in, but I point this out, because in the next part, I will be taking apart something the child's father said in court, not in spite, more a case of how he may have been convinced by the police, I had murdered his child and "Someone needed to pay for his sorrow" but I am not calling him a liar, just how he was mistaken.

*　　*　　*　　*　　*

Cumberland News. 21st April. 1961. Pages 1 & 15.

Twenty Eight witnesses, including four children gave evidence yesterday during the first day of the hearing at Carlisle County Magistrates Court of a murder charge against a 17 year old youth.

Mr Warwick said he was returning to work about 1.10 p.m. on March 4 when he saw his son with the accused near the hospital powerhouse. *1.

Four children aged between seven and ten years, said they saw Peck several times on Saturday afternoon.

They were given a special stand so they could see over the top of the witness box.

All four listened intently as the clerk, Mr James Stables, explained the oath to them and they gave their evidence audibly and clearly.

One of the boys said the last time Peck spoke to them, he said he was going to make some bows and arrows. George Warwick and Aidan Murphy said they would go with him, but Aidan came back. The last time he saw George was when he was walking up to the farm with Peck. *2.

Another of George's playmates said he last saw George walking hand in hand with Peck in the direction of the farm. *3.

A jigsaw of circumstantial evidence pointed clearly how George was murdered, said Mr Wood.

The various pieces of evidence by themselves might not appear to say much, but when put together one gets a very clear picture, he said. Mr Wood alleged that the picture points overwhelmingly to Peck.

Peck has denied throughout that he was responsible for the little boy's death, he added.

[Some of these statements are repeats, but worthy of being reported here.]

On the afternoon it happened, Peck was seen in the farm yard with some young boys including George.

At 4.10 p.m. he was seen talking to three girls at a sand heap, near where the body was found. Between then and 4.30 p.m. he returned to where the young boys were and asked them if they wanted to make a bow and arrow.

Peck and the murdered boy were seen walking together near to where the body was later found, alleged Mr Wood. The accused was next seen in a ward at the hospital at 4.45 p.m. *4

When questioned Peck said he had left the "little ginger boy" at the corner of the laundry and gone in for tea.

Peck appears to have been the last person seen with George Warwick and there was a great deal of scientific evidence, he alleged.

There was also blood on the side of his shoes. When this was examined on the day after the little boy's death, it was still wet. *5

He left the school before the laundry came and it was a custom for the staff to give you some clothing from a number not in use if you were short, the prosecution said.

Next there was the evidence of a small piece of thread said Mr Wood, Peck had a bath after the date when the harvester had been and no foreign matter was found on him then.*6

*　　　*　　　*　　　*　　　*

The article is almost a complete reproduction, word for word of what was recorded in the previous days paper, I am not sure if this was the editors idea or the prosecution brainwashing the jury, it's too exact!

It's a good thing Juries "Never" read the daily or evening papers, before a hearing, let alone during a trial, having no knowledge of the case, means that the court found 12 men and women, all of whom had never read the local or regional newspapers…so the question should be asked, were they from Outer Mongolia or from the local home for geriatrics?

And just in the Interest of British Justice, under no circumstances, let them have access to all the documents and statements of qualified experts.

*1. If we return to Monday March 6th. 1961. [Cover] It stated: "His father is understood to have seen his son talking to a man in the clothes of a hospital patient…"

Both statements taken together will make more sense, but add a bit of confusion, as to who the "ginger haired boy" was.

The father saw his son talking to a "man" at the powerhouse, When I recently returned to Garlands, I asked where the powerhouse was, it turned out, it used to be on the road leading up to the hospital, quite a long distance from the farm, where I had been playing with some boys in the barn, I was quoted as saying; "One was the farmer's son." [Second police statement R13] Okay so the police knew the dead boy was the farmer's son, but I did not know that and according to the father, his son was at the powerhouse at precisely the same time, so once again why didn't the police make either any search for the "Ginger haired boy?" I had been playing with or had they already found him, but that would have been too inconvenient under the circumstances, come to that why didn't the jury ask the same question.

Another point being, I feel it is a safer bet to suggest the father recognised his own son at the powerhouse and the statement by the police was another invention, to try to have me with the boy in the farm at the same time I was almost 17 years old, I did not shave, had no acne or anything else to give the impression of being anything other than a young teenager, the distance from the road to the powerhouse was less than 20 feet, the father was only 30 years old, so it can be taken for granted, a 17 year old boy could not be mistaken as a man, at such a short distance, unless he had stubble on his chin or long sideburns and not wearing the clothing of a patient.

Compared to a patients clothing, my own clothing was very modern, except when I was in court, my own clothing having been taken from me, I was then wearing patients clothing, so what did the father see in court a young teenager or someone wearing hospital clothing in the court room?

Back to two statements, one the father recognised his son at the powerhouse, but I had a witness that at the same time, recognised me Mr John Paton, who was also the nurse on my ward [second police statement] 13R. To 14Q. Talking about seeing the nurse arrive with his daughter, just after we had left the farm and I was heading to the bus stop, that couldn't be seen from the farm, but I had also pointed out that I saw the bus coming; hence I was in the square.

I have just thought of how the laundry may have come into the police statements, it could be possible that someone had told the police, the boy had been seen at the laundry with a man at 4.15 p.m., but at the same time were not prepared to state on oath, exactly who they saw, because they just observed it without taking much notice, pity really because, they too would have pointed out the guy was wearing patients clothing.

The fact that I had admitted talking to the boys, playing with some others and on speaking to the group of boys to make arrangements for the next day, not taking much notice of who followed me for 50 feet , whilst I had something else on my mind, like filling in some holes and looking for eggs, plus the police initially getting two other witnesses to suggest I had been seen by them 10 minutes before the bus left or like the blood on my shoe during the interview on the Saturday, I knew there was blood on my shoe, I just didn't know it had been removed and substituted with the child's blood.

So it wasn't, my statement about being anywhere near the laundry, so much for the doctor's same statement implying I had, it was the child who had been seen at the laundry, so it was then added I claimed it was myself, which in later press reports, will be seen I did not even mention the laundry only the O.T.

*2. Okay this has been pointed out several times in previous chapters, but it was impossible to say which direction I had taken, once I reached the end of the path, going left behind the church, I appreciate they were young children in the witness box and obviously "fairly well rehearsed" in what they had to say.

*3. This is even more obvious if we return to reading his statement, in the Cumberland News, 21st April 1961. *2. In which it stated that; "Peck and George walked away hand in hand in the direction of the hospital farm." As Aidan Murphy said; "The last time he saw George was when he was walking up to the farm with Peck."

They were all in a den in some bushes, first behind the O.T. building, and then apparently front of the hospital, maybe they were nomads, but whose eyes were observing this and were they all trust worthy policemen?

Now if we return to the first chapter covering the Statements, No.11 we discover Richard Hall aged 7, "10 weeks" earlier had said; "that two of his friends had followed me towards "The Church!" and "Not the Farm!"

*4. Where did this wet blood on the side of my shoe come from, it wasn't there when the shoes were examined the next morning, only some inside the toe of the shoe and in the pattern work on top of the shoe.

*5. Note the difference between a thread of a button that falls off, takes a lot longer to release itself, than by being scientifically cut and gently pulled out of the material.

The next reports are from the Trial, in both the Daily and Evening Papers.

For some reason there wasn't any daily reports, only one on the 19th May 1961, there may well have been, but glancing through, the chances are they said the same thing as the evening paper, so to save cost I didn't copy them out...I was on a very tight budget to photocopy everything.

Cumberland Evening News, Wednesday May 17.1961. P.1. [cover].

It opens; "Unless and until the defence proves otherwise, the jury at the trial, at Cumberland Assizes, Carlisle, of M J W Peck were told today by prosecution counsel that they must presume, he is sufficiently sane to be answerable in law for the murder which it is alleged he committed.

A report of the opening of the trial yesterday appears on page 3.

At the resumption of the trial, this morning, Mr Glover said that in addition to the handkerchiefs, button and thread, which had been referred to the previous day. Seminal stains were discovered on the trousers and underpants and on the trousers of George Warwick. These stains had been caused by a secretor of blood group A. *1.

A number of male nurses at the hospital would be giving evidence. They would say that they never heard of or saw any signs of recent injury which could have accounted for the considerable quantity of blood found on the accused's shoe and sock.

"At the time that this offence was committed." said Mr Glover, "the accused was a patient at Garlands; therefore You must be asking yourselves, if it was the accused who committed this dreadful crime, what was his state of mind at the time? Was he sane or insane? Until the matter was raised by the defence, he suggested that whilst listening to the evidence, they should keep the question at the back of their minds." *2.

One of the dead boy's playmates, seven year old Richard Hall, giving evidence to-day in a firm clear voice told how he and his friends were playing in a den amongst some bushes opposite the front of the hospital. Peck was there and said he was going to make some bows and arrows and asked who would come with him. *3

At first a boy called Aiden said he would go, but it was George Warwick that went. Peck and George walked away hand in hand in the direction of the hospital farm. That was the last time he saw George.

A male nurse Thomas Ellwood said he was on duty during the afternoon of March 4. Between 4.45 and 4.50 p.m. he noticed Peck watching television; he had not seen him earlier.

Cross examined by Mr Glynn Burrell he agreed that he had been busy attending 40 to 50 patients in various parts of the ward. He had not seen Peck enter the room.*4.

Page 3. Mr Glover told the jury in his opening address: "The crime and circumstances of it are horrifying. They may stress you to the limits of your endurance. I regret that I cannot spare you the details of the crime. You have been called to perform a most important public duty. That duty is to steel yourself to listen to the evidence and to judge it calmly and dispassionately.

The accursed youth was a patient at the Garlands Hospital. The people who go there are in many different degrees of mental illness, he said it was not thought any particular security was needed for Peck, he was allowed to wander about the hospital grounds and farm buildings as he wished.

The Q.C. said that the evidence "points without doubt to the accursed as the guilty man."

Peck had been a boarder at Edmond Castle School and allocated number 42. No.30 had been given to another boy. This was not Peck's number, but of the boys who had it, one had been at Garlands as a patient 15 months before the crime and the other boy had not been at the hospital.

It appears that the handkerchief No.30 had got muddled and Peck got it in addition to his own when he left to go to the hospital. *5.

There was evidence of one completely clean trouser button which was found in the pen, close to where the boy's battered body was found.

The button was clean whilst the pen where it was found was dirty. No.6.

They were seen 200 yards from where the body of the boy was found. So far as any prosecution witness was concerned, that was the last time George Warwick was alive.

Describing the scene Mr Glover said: "There they went hand in hand together the young man of 16 and the boy of 4." The boy's body was found at 9.15 p.m. he was quite dead, said Mr Glover. "He was half naked, His hands tied behind his back with string and he had been sexually assaulted, He had been battered to death, by blows from some blunt instrument on the head. Those were harsh, brutal and inescapable facts. *7.

Medical evidence would be given to prove that the boy died between 4 p.m. and 6 p.m. The time can be narrowed further, however, because Peck was seen near the farm buildings at about 3.50 and by about 4.45 he was back in his ward.*8.

*   *   *   *   *

*1. Hold it a moment, who decided that the seminal stains on the boy, were mine? Considering when my clothing was taken away and it was apparent I had not had a bath or washed my genital area, because the report on my examination and clothing, by a doctor who took swabs from me, plus pathologist and a forensic scientist, pointed out there was no sexual matter on myself or on the thread found within my foreskin.

*2. Sounds like he is saying; concentrate on his insanity, it will help blind you to whatever else is being said.

*3. Note how the den suddenly became; "Opposite the Front of the Hospital" from where it would have been very possible to see someone walking to the farm…but therein lies a problem that would make their den opposite to the sand heap, which was opposite the hospital entrance, plus the 3 girls, the eldest of which was Philomena were never invited repeatedly to give evidence to contradict a 7 year old boy, whose den kept moving around and neither was the farm worker William Johnson called a second time who saw me talking to the girls, but then he becomes a bit suspicious, considering he had allowed himself to be persuaded to claim it was 25 minutes earlier or 10 minutes before the bus left. Maybe Philomena stuck to the facts and couldn't be encouraged to lie, hence an unreliable witness for the police and prosecution.

*4. This nurse was handing out medication to 40 to 50 patients, so the only patients he recalled seeing, were those he was looking for, I was not on any form of medication, so why should he look for me, I was probably having my tea, plus the tele-caster came on at 4.41 as I sat down to watch the program I wanted to see, plus if you return to Launder's statement I did not say Southend had won or lost, I just joked that they Always win/never loose, look at it this way, if you arrange to meet someone in a crowded pub, how many strangers do you actually see when looking for your friends, you just notice they are not the person, but don't "see" them, let alone describe them.

*5. Muddled? When was this decided? Before or after it was discovered during the inquest, that items of clothing and hankies, were only given to boys, if the number was not allocated to anyone else…Re: 20.4.61. Plus let's go back to Launder's first statement 59R. Why would the school give me an extra hanky, after convincing me I would be returning the same night! They obviously didn't give me any other clothing, so why an extra hanky, that miraculously bore the same number of a boy who had been there 15 months earlier. It's a pity it wasn't reported how the matron had an argument in the court that hankies were not numbered in biro, but Indian ink or had the press also made up their minds I was guilty, so such trivia would have been unimportant.

*6. If ever I return to the Lord Chancellors Office, with someone with a good camera, you will see the button is on top of a bag of dry cement, yet it fell into a drainage channel, so did it then rise up to the bag of cement, after the police claimed it was next to the boy's body [there were lots of documents that had gone brown with age that could not be photocopied, but a digital camera would pick up. Note it was me who volunteered where I had lost it, when it was implied it was in the pig's sty, before I was told where it had been found.

*7. Not overlooking the inescapable facts; that the string in my pockets and locker, were different from that which the boys hands were tied up with, plus the medical evidence pointing out I had not recently indulged in any sexual activities, prior to the examination or the estimated time of the boy's death.

*8. It appears that quite a lot of witnesses saw me near the farm buildings, including 3 girls and a farm worker, all of which vouched for the fact I was on my own, when heading towards the farm, plus a witness who did not appear in court, who could vouch for my being on my own when crossing the road to the church [the German artist], plus the person I had spent the afternoon with or the bus driver who could have confirmed he left the hospital at 4 p.m., regardless of one or two peoples claims, that it had been at the very least 10 minutes later.

I remember once after an accident, I was asked to ,make a statement, that wasn't exactly what the police wanted to hear, I was kept at the station for several hours "just in case" my details of the event could be closer to their version of what other people claimed…obviously they did not know who I was, but they eventually let me go home and said I would be hearing from them, that oddly enough they failed to do…which may explain why there are very few eye-witnesses in large crowds or could it be they too were kept in a police station for hours on end…

I will just cover two more sections, including the summing up of the trial, but as said several times, You the readers, can make your own decisions on how safe our legal system is, because unlike juries at all major and minor trials, if they want a patsy…You or your children can become a victim of the law, but hopefully you now have enough information to protect yourselves and families, from those sick perverts who make it possible, to destroy people's lives.

But in this case, you have an advantage, in so far as you are aware of the original statements and expert opinions, to compare just how corrupt those who are supposed to be protecting children and victims of violent crimes are…it would seem to be a game, that's made even more exciting, by holding the trump card, that gives protection to all those perverts in the form of; whatever they say or do, they will be protected for 75 years, during which time everyone involved, may die hence end of story…the facts in this case…are supposedly to be kept as an official secret until I am 92 years old or to be more precise 2036, when those two statements by Launder, will be read as written, with apparently no one to question the stupidity and constant lies throughout them.

If anything good comes out of this, then it will help a great many people, especially those yet to be born with bladders that fail to disconnect at birth.

The main purpose of this story was to write about what life was like, for someone growing up with severe incontinence…obviously they had no idea what lay within Pandora's Box…but one thing I will Never claim is that; My Life Has Been Unique, because if it happened to me, then it can happen to anyone…if not precisely, then at least large parts of it and don't forget, for as long as psychologist are given the protection of not being cross examined in courts or everyday life, where mere postulations of those who help bring about laws, to protect child molesters, justify incest or any other form of sexual depravity…there will never be freedom or protection for any members of society.

Plus if I hadn't had a Friendly Q.C. who tried to convince me to destroy large parts of the original book, because anyone who has studied the law in depth will know immediately it was pure fiction.

Now if a retired High Court Judge was unaware of how easy it is to frame a victim of the system and then do a complete cover-up, then what chance does Joe Blogs have?

Okay I admit I have a few problems caused in part to a set of principles and I don't like to be put down or accused of being a liar, which had I been a liar…none of these closely guarded secrets would have ever seen the light of day, until 2036.

So onwards into the valley of death they rode or however the poem goes, I will cover the two sections as promised, if you wish to read more, then you have the names of the newspapers and more importantly the dates of publication, so you can glean them for yourselves, in either Carlisle Public Library or the British Museum Library [BML] in Hendon.

*   *   *   *   *

The Cumberland News 19.5.61 states more or less what had been stated in all its previous editions, adding just a few observations of what took place.

A sack stained with blood was not of human origin. Peck had told the police that he had wiped his shoe with a sack at the farm. *1.

"Evidence given by Peck"

Peck when he went into the witness box yesterday afternoon, gave evidence in a low voice and had to be asked several times to speak up. He described what happened when he left the children on March 4.

"I walked away towards the church. There were two boys following me. One had a "Y" shaped pattern on his jeans. The other boy who I called "Ginger" wore maroon trousers. *2

I said something to them about bows and arrows. One of the boys went back, I said to "Ginger": "Aren't you going back? I put my hand in my pocket and he got hold of my sleeve."

An ambulance had passed by and he got hold of the boy's hand and pulled him to one side.

"I said I was going in for my tea. He asked for a biscuit and if I was going to make bows and arrows. I told him to come along tomorrow.

"He stood still when I walked away and I did not see him again. I took a short cut through the bushes. If he had followed me he would have fallen into the ditch."

Peck said he was going to fill in some holes, where he had dug up some plants. *3.

After attending to the flowers he spoke to some little girls, and then he walked along to the workshops, and went back to his ward. He visited the toilet, washed his hands and went upstairs. He sat and watched television.

Peck said he did not return to the farm yard. After leaving George Warwick on the roadway, "I never seen him again" *4.

He had a trouser button missing for a week before March 4. He had lost it in the slaughterhouse. He had not been told where the boy's body had been found. "I was just told they had some things in evidence".

He said the semen stains on his underpants occurred on the Thursday; there had been a dance on the Wednesday night.

"I did nothing to harm the little boy. I did not hit him on the head with a brick," declared Peck.

*1. So it is obvious the jury, didn't accept the police deception either, but we don't know why the hankies in the bucket, were not handed in to Cliff or Corby or could it be they were considered as actual evidence…earlier they claimed I had said they weren't mine, then searched for a witness to say they weren't mine, why? After taking them to the bucket, where I had put them to soak, but then what happened on that night, the jury was kept well in the dark about.

*2. These things were in a cellophane bag in the witness box to help me remember…maybe it sounds like a wild accusation, but think about it this way, I apparently managed to remember the design on a boys trousers, ten weeks after the occasion of only ever seeing him briefly and to my knowledge, but I could describe one item of clothing, but nothing else about him, unlike the ginger haired boy who I had seen a lot, what with picking him up to see into the pens or throwing up the hay stack, also the fact that the boy who was murdered, was some distance away observed by his father, when playing with his kids.

*3. This is interesting, having nicked some plants for my visitor, I returned to hide the evidence, now think about it, if I had enough sense to cover my tracks where a few plants were concerned, then wouldn't it make sense, that had I killed anyone in a pen, I would have removed the button, hanky or hankies and any other evidence? Think about it this way; if I was an apparently a cold blooded psychopath who had just murdered a child and casually walked back to the ward to watch television, without a care in the world or do psychopaths only feel guilty about nicking flowers, but not to murdering young boys. Oh come off it, only a student of psychology, would accept that line of reasoning!

*4. This was probably [like most of these reports are an interpretation of a reporter, considering everything I said in the witness box, seems to imply I had only been questioned for a few minutes] the only time I had inadvertently told a lie, based I would think on how the police had repeatedly asked me, if I had returned to the farm and Launder trying to prove that after going to the farm, I had returned later with the boy, who had vanished before the girls returned to where the kids were playing, but the child was not with them, therefore I would have been compelled to search the hospital grounds for him...it was well gone 4 o'clock. He could have gone home for his tea, but it seems according to Launder I made a frantic search for that One Child.

*　　*　　*　　*　　*

Southend and Country Pictorial. May 19. 1961.

Dr J C Menzies said he had examined Peck at 11.15 p.m. on the day the child died, there was no blood on him, but he did notice a scab on his left ankle, about one inch long and half an inch wide.

Peck was interviewed by D/Sgt Albert Launder of Carlisle, who had taken note of his movements and questioned him about George Warwick who was then missing.

Peck had told him that he was playing with eight children in the bushes during the afternoon, he had left them and two followed him. One went back, but the other one who Peck called Kidda followed him to the corner of the laundry.*1.

Dr A Cliff told the court that blood staining on Peck's trousers and the handkerchiefs which he found near the child's body were similar to Peck's. *2.

Peck in the witness box, said he had lived in children's homes, since he was 18 months old. "I have no parents now, he said, all in all he added, he had lived 14 years in children's homes and three months in approved schools.

His defence counsel Mr Glyn Burrell, Q.C. asked him if there were any young children at the homes where he stayed and would he have done anything to harm them.

Peck replied that he liked small children and would not harm them.

Mr Burrell opening the case for the defence, said there were two main questions, "Who murdered the little boy and the state of Peck's mind."

From D/Sgt Launder's very fair and exhaustive evidence of the accused movements on the day in question, it could been seen that his account of them were consistent throughout.

Mr Burrell went on; "If you are sure that this boy is the killer, but when he did it he was suffering from an abnormality of the mind which subsequently impaired his responsibility for his acts, then the right verdict for you to bring in would be one of manslaughter."

The defence evidence, which would be called would be that he was suffering from a psychopathic disorder.*3.

*1. One does not have to return to either of Launder's statements to know that I had never implied that I had been playing with eight children in the bushes, during the afternoon, but had pointed out that I had a visitor, plus I feel Mr Burrell's statement that Launder very fair statement, is a typing error, so instead of saying; "That Launder's account of them was consistent throughout, it should read…he was a consistent liar throughout" snag is no one knew the evidence, except 3 Q.C's one of which kept thinking they were all on the same side…

*2. Similar in what way, they came from someone who was a blood secretor? But 40% of the population [according to Cliff] had group A secretor blood. Also he found farmyard dust and chaff in my trouser turn ups, similar to that on the farm I went to daily and would probably be found on a whole list of farms.

*3. Well at least I had some people on my side, it's a pity none of them were wearing wigs or the initials Q.C. after their names, what sort of defence council would start his opening statement with what was the state of Peck's mind, before going on to describe the person he was defending, as having an abnormality of the mind? And what scientific knowledge was he relying on… the fact I had incontinence, it's enough to make a person wonder how many incontinent people were sent to the gallows, because they were psychopath's and liable to become schizophrenics!

*   *   *   *   *

Now although the next one is dated the 25th, it was a weekly paper, but is being put in now before the Cumberland Evening News, as it covers the same events of 19th of May.

Southend Standard. Thurs. May 25. 1961. P.12.

After a four day trial, Malcolm Peck a 17 year old, mental hospital patient was found guilty at Cumberland Assizes, Carlisle, on Friday of murdering four year old George Taylor Warwick in the hospital grounds.

On the grounds of diminished responsibility and sentenced to life imprisonment.

Mr Justice Veale told Peck it was "a dreadful crime."

Peck retorted, "I didn't do it" and had to be removed from the dock by three prison officers.

When the trial resumed on Friday, Dr L O W Pickering [senior medical officer at Durham Prison] said no signs of insanity had been detected in Peck, but he said he did not think Peck was able to control his actions.

Dr Pickering agreed that Peck in reports by medical officers at various institutions, had been described as "a seriously maladjusted boy," "unable to take his place in society," "seriously hampered by feelings of insecurity and inadequacy" ""neurotic" and "having a marked difference between his intelligence and the use he makes of it."

Mr Glyn Burrell. Q.C. [defence] said the evidence pointed away from Peck. *1.

Should the jury consider Peck's mental fitness, the evidence of Dr Pickering was unchallenged.

[The rest of the item is the same as the previous one except this small part during the time I was in the box.]

He said: "I lived for awhile with my stepfather and his wife, but I was not happy there, they treated me like a dog instead of a human being." *2.

*1. Well at least he saw the facts for what they were, but obviously blinded himself to the reality, that being in a mental hospital, because in cold weather I would get severe headaches after being repeatedly beaten unconscious, via high heeled shoes, lumps of wood, slashed with knives etcetera, I was not on any medication, just unobserved observation, for after all is said and done, why work, when he had so many expert reports by others of his same ilk, who just quoted other people's opinions, on someone they had met for an hour, with preconceived opinions, disregarding a life time of apprehensions of those in authority, unlike the doctor in Runwell who got through to me, after several interviews and found all previous statements, contradicted the reality. Hence being under general observation in a mental hospital, did not make me a lunatic, but he seemed to imply to the jury: "That anyone in their right minds, would never challenge the findings of a medical officer so; Guilty or Not, who wants an inadequate psychopath running around in society, who's to say he may not be capable of being guilty of an actual murder, in years to come?"

*2. I am sure I did not say "I was not happy there, but then there is another small point to take into consideration, and that is just before going into the witness box, he told the court about my life with my stepmother and I recall how I had tried not to listen, as the memories took over, I was prepared to stand up in the witness box and have my say, but he destroyed my defences, which will explain why I was repeatedly asked to speak louder, also all these years later I cannot control my emotions when she comes into conversations, but at the time of my trial they had happened very recently, plus another point being, that throughout my life, whenever I had been accused of something I had not done, I would panic because they were usually of things I could not prove I had not done, knowing at the time, I was about to be punished severely, plus more often than not, not allowed to say anything, which came under; speaking back, that in turn demanded more punishments, even now, 50 odd years later I panic and go into states of depression, if it is implied I am guilty of something I have not done…maybe it's the panic on my face, that is interpreted as being guilty until I find a way of proving otherwise… one of my girl-friends joked at a party that I had raped her, I panicked, couldn't speak and went home with tears running down my face and almost on the point of committing suicide, rather than be locked away again, it was only when the joke [?] reached a friend who knew a lot about my history, heard what had happened, did he get in his car and intercepted me before I got home, although I really liked the woman, I made sure never to be alone with her again and stopped seeing and talking to her.

Maybe he was trying to use the postulation of psychologist, that battered children beat their own children, when they grow up and start a family…I am sure my daughter or my friends can vouch for the fact I rarely ever hit her, except as a last resort and being violently attacked by her, which always ended up suffering a great deal more than she did, because I always remembered what it had been like for myself, plus although whenever I did hit her, usually because it was a spontaneous reaction and she did not run fast enough, those times were the only times, she gave me any affection, but I was not going to spend my life beating her up to get respect…although had I known the future, I should have paid someone and had her put down…

Only a person who is a pervert and a convincing compulsive liar, will use such a sick excuse as; "It was because they were beaten without mercy every day, when they themselves were children" That they beat their kids Now!

Sounds a bit too much like another jewish excuse for committing genocide in Palestine, well the German's tried to exterminate all the jews, who were promoting incest and paedophilia and other totally depraved postulations of jewish psychology, that after the war, the jews felt compelled to destroy the lives of everyone who did not, support incest and paedophilia, but as this book is pointing out, it would seem that those; who make the laws to protect themselves and persecute the innocent , back that Zionist Nazi State, that even their own gods threw them out of to wander the world for eternity, and all those idiots [and child molesting religions] who claim to worship the denounced [by the other gods] god of the jews, but then created a Zionist State, okay some people may claim it was mythology about the God of the Jews casting them out of the Holy Lands. But the curse of 4 generations, being imposed on anyone offending All Gods, seem to have come about or is it merely a coincidence, that every country where child pornography is considered as a mere misdemeanour are the closest allies of them, supplying them with weapons, the means of building nuclear weapons, food and a blind eye to all that quagmire's violations of human rights, when they cry, oh but it was because of the holocaust or how they are persecuted everywhere they go, overlooking if they did not promote paedophilia and genocide everywhere they went throughout history, the holocaust would never have happened, note it was just the paedophiles, who were predominantly students of Freudian psychology, that were taken to the extermination camps, so they only have themselves to blame, when it turned out that the bulk of those perverts just so happened to be jews, with a subconscious desire to be exterminated, plus from the great numbers of Jews who lived in Germany throughout the entire war, it was obvious Hitler had hitherto had no problems with jews, just nonce cases of which the majority turned out to be jews.

Who on earth came up with the postulation, that everyone tortured as a child, will only ever torturer their own or other people's children, you may as well make it compulsory to sterilise anyone who has been a victim of violence, when it is the violent people that should be sterilised… kiddy fiddlers should have their hands chopped of immediately and foreheads branded with an "N" then refused medical treatment, but if they request a day out in a famous beauty spot where people love to jump to their deaths, then be compassionate enough to take them there.

But it is usually the arguments mainly used by; "The SS" [social services] who it would seem from the large numbers of social workers in prison for beating up and sexually assaulting children in "Their Care", that to be a social worker it is a requirement; not only to have studied Freud, without questioning any of his stupidities, but to have been beaten and raped by their own parents or legal guardians.

Cumberland Evening News. Saturday, May 20th 1961. P.3.

A 17 year old, mental hospital patient struggled with three warders in the dock at Cumberland Assizes, in Carlisle last night, when he was sentenced to life imprisonment for the manslaughter of a four year old boy.

As he was forced down the steps Malcolm John William Peck cried repeatedly: "I didn't do it---I didn't do it."

Peck, c/o Garlands Mental Hospital, Carlisle, was found guilty of the manslaughter of George Taylor Warwick on March 4, in the grounds of the hospital farm.

The jury after being out for exactly 30 minutes returned a verdict that Peck was not guilty of murder but guilty of manslaughter on grounds of diminished responsibility.

Mr Justice Veale, passing sentence told him: "You have been convicted of a dreadful crime, I have no doubt that the jury are right in saying at the time your mental responsibility was diminished."

"But you knew what you were doing." His Lordship continued "and knew that it was wrong."

He did not consider that this was a case for exercise of his powers under the 1959 Mental Health Act. If Peck's mental state required treatment the authorities had power to order that he should have it.

My duty is to protect the public…the sentence I am about to pass on you will be periodically reviewed. The sentence is imprisonment for life, concluded His Lordship.

The two warders, who had sat beside Peck since Tuesday afternoon, when the trial opened, motioned him to move down the steps. He began to struggle and a third officer was needed to restrain him.

He cried: "I didn't do it—I didn't do it" as he was taken down the steps to the cells. Twice more from below the dock he could be heard still crying "I didn't do it."

* * * * *

The greatest shock being, I was convinced that under British Justice, no one is found guilty for crimes they have not committed, plus for 2 days on the journeys back and forth from the prison to the court and back, my escorts were convinced I would be back at the school soon and were completely baffled by the results and convinced along those lines, was probably the first time I had lowered my defences, hence crying that I had not done it...

My Friendly Q.C. who years later, helped me find the evidence, observed that guilty people in his experience, no matter how hard they fought for their freedom, accepted a guilty verdict, by shrugging their shoulders.

Okay I should be slightly fairer to the jury, who after four days of hearing about "my apparent state of mind" being constantly reminded that I was in a mental hospital and the words psychopath and schizophrenic were repeatedly used [no I am not going to count the numbers of times they were implied] were obviously used to brainwash them, especially when my so-called defence kept pointing it out as well , plus Dr Pickering's unquestioned findings, the bulk of which were plagiarised from other like-minded reports.

Maybe you noticed not much of Launder's had been questioned either, adding to this My Q.C. although he had pointed out all the evidence pointed away from me, had gone out of his way to convince the jury; that I was a psychopath anyway and the fact he told me not to Appeal until he had come to see me, and I have never heard nor seen him since, leaves very little for anyone to wonder what his own opinions were, about approved school boys in mental hospitals.

It is also a pity the judge's words were quoted by dashes, when what he said has stayed in my mind all these years:

"You have been found guilty on circumstantial evidence, which means; that although this court has not produced enough evidence to say you committed this crime, You haven't produced enough evidence to Prove that You did not Commit This Crime."

In other words: "British Justice means: You are Guilty until You can Prove Yourself Innocent" but every effort will be made to prevent you from doing so... hey wait a moment, isn't the fantasy supposed to be: "Everyone is Presumed to be Innocent, Until Proven Guilty?

The fact that in the judges report, it states the time of the bus leaving has been confirmed, so why did he not query, why it was so important for Launder to have me everywhere else 10-20 minutes, before it was humanly possible, I had 9 witnesses, but only 4 appeared in court for the prosecution, they were the 3 girls and a farm labourer, who confirmed I was on my own...it was in a large area without many trees or bushes around it, although after Aiden Murphy had moved his den 3 times, he must have taken the bushes with him.

Plus the person who had been with me from 1.30 p.m. to 4 p.m. wasn't called as a witness and neither was any reference made to her, accept when she took her cat into the court room then evicted, plus according to the Lord Chancellors Office, she was not asked to make a statement, also none of the witnesses I had pointed out, were not requested to make statements or give evidence, so who was my Court Appointed Q.C. working for and was I his first case?

Okay so the Press cannot be relied on to write all the facts, but what they did report was more or less, what the jury heard…twisted statements that contradicted Launder's statements, a lot of the forensic reports, nothing about how anyone can get blood only on the toe of a sock and wet blood inside the toe of the shoe, without any blood being on any other part of both the sock and the shoe. Plus they kept pointing out a button and a hanky being next to the child's body that had been moved to the farm office, before he was reported as being found…maybe he was not found in the slaughterhouse, then there were the mittens found on a low wall inside the slaughterhouse, not handed over to forensics, did they have blood on them, plus why tie up a 4 year old boys hands or was this also done later…oh and we already know the state of Launder's mind, when he opened his statement: "Now Malcolm you have given us one account of what happened on Saturday… you remember Saturday don't you…obviously in his determination to corrupt the evidence, he had overlooked trying to find out if I was on medication…which I wasn't, then how many times was an old wound on my ankle, referred to… that I had acquired before going to the nut house and nothing to do with the case…or was this another ploy to distract the jury.

But I feel sure you will recognise all the obstacles put in my way, to prevent a fair trial in any sense of the word, if it were not for the jury's presence, it could have been given its correct name, i.e. Police State Kangaroo Court!

Oh yeah who was that mysterious farm worker, who turned up in court 10 weeks after the crime, who claimed to have seen me walking with the boy, pass the same place as the girls were playing, but claimed he never saw the girls or the other farm labourer, less than half the distance from where he was, plus the point that to have been able to see the sand heap from that distance, he had to be in or very close to the slaughterhouse, there isn't a statement by him either in the Lord Chancellors Office and did he have a reputation for interfering with children.

Although just out of curiosity I would like to know whatever happened to the ginger-haired boy, surely the other two children he was playing with at the lunch-time in the barn, must have told the police who he was…just in case you have forgotten, he was the little boy I was playing with, just before going to meet my visitor and the murdered child was seen some way off, in a different direction and observed by the father, as a man, wearing hospital clothing.

Well if nothing else comes of this case, at least you now know how easy it is for the Defence counsel and the police to pull the wool over a jury's eyes, plus you are guilty of any crime a zealous/dubious copper throws at you, by withholding evidence…but then how many people get to see all the statements before it goes to court and recorded by the press, not overlooking everything was supposed to have been hidden away, with a 75 year ban on the public ever knowing the truth, well maybe that should read; "Not knowing the Truth behind what was handed over to the LCO, that looked very clever and would have remained unquestioned, had I died in the meantime and not questioned or figured it out, and yep it wasn't that easy, until too many questions and answers failed to make sense, a point that was hard to see at a glance and if I hadn't had a Q.C. [I could have done with at the time of the trial] I would never have discovered anything, but there again, he was convinced for a couple of years, my story was a work of fiction, and I am not a liar or like to be accused of lying either, but at least the book 1984, [well the film]…inadvertently showed me how to get the initial evidence.

Oh all that information was being gathered to take it to the Court of Appeal before a couple of Government Officials called at my home one night, to remind me of my only condition for discharge, to not try to take any evidence to the Appeal court, otherwise I would be returned to Broadmoor for further treatment, for an imaginary psychological illness, that although you have never had it, doesn't mean that in the otherwise unforeseeable future, such a state of mind could exist and become known as "Greck's Syndrome" which will cover all the innocent people, who find it impossible to accept the "Psychologically Disturbed Postulations of British Justice."

Plus if I am seen anywhere near the Royal Courts of Appeal., I would be arrested, regardless of the fact my operation was conclusive proof I was not a psychopath and never likely to become schizophrenic…arguments put forward by; "Unquestionable Psychiatrist" as the reason for suffering with incontinence, which was what caused this book to come about, well the first half of it anyway…

Well my not being an Authority on the Postulations of Delusions, that have to be accepted as self-evident, then the only conclusion can be, is that: "Insanity is caused by an Innocent Person's Desire to Seek the Truth!"

It will take another couple of chapters to explain how those Officials found out I was going to the Appeal Courts and how with their help indirectly the rest of my life has been destroyed, wow if I wasn't eccentric I would have become a psychopath and maybe life would have been easier and not resulted in the lives of a couple of more children's lives being destroyed , even though they never were incontinent and one more case of evidence, to try to bring about a new law to protect children and adults from another evil crime sanctioned by "Her Britannic Majesties Law Makers", to protect nonce cases, come to think about it there are a lot more Laws to protect Paedophiles, than there are to protect children from them…regardless of if they are wearing plain or blue uniforms, and don't forget there are 4 different forms of paedophiles, those who rape children, those who condone the raping of children by looking the other way and the lowest forms of life, who would rather frame an innocent person, to protect those freaks who murder children.

Oh yes, maybe I should in one small way, appreciate a law that was designed to protect evil bastards, who go around beating people up with immunity from prosecution, on the grounds they are psychologically disturbed, because if that sick law had never come about to protect societies terrorist, I would never have been able to use a tongue in cheek threat against a G.P. who had been refusing to, maybe on paedophile supporting arguments, that incontinence was all in my mind and I would only be wasting the time of a urologist…the rest is history, except there are times I wish I had never had the operation, what with better discreet incontinence wear coming onto the market, but then it was hard going into a specialist shop for such protection, because of the "knowing" looks and sniggers, due making it obvious, I was suffering with a disturbed mind…no matter how hard it was to convince a medical expert…that can never be seen to be wrong, that my experiments and years of observations, implied otherwise, plus I would never have learnt I was not unique and better still never have been asked to write a book about what my life had been like, due to incontinence, okay I would still have an evil daughter, but I could have shared my beautiful grandchildren's lives, as I went into 4th childhood, albeit at a slower pace, plus never having the SS putting me on trial in my absence and given an even worse punishment.

I also have spent my life with a couple of other strange phobias, one caused by being told by people who were ex-Broadmoor patients, who had gone to visit friends and then refused to be allowed to return home on the flimsiest excuses, that they knew they would be returning, because they kept dreaming about being returned…dreams I have been having for years, but although the dreams were of another time, they also were about begging to be with my daughter and later grandchildren and offering to sign any statements, just to go home again…weird memories that played a part I suppose that kept me almost out of trouble, except when accused or having it implied I may have done something, I would go into panic mode…but then as with the day I got out, I dressed in weird clothing, even if wearing a 3 piece suit, one item would clash, just to make sure someone would remember me if I needed a witness, but then I didn't have to pretend to be eccentric, too many people kept telling me I am!

Over the last few years I have been having strange, but at times strangely funny dreams about being dead and once [although sort of knowing a dream is just that, a dream] felt so happy I decided not to wake up, but just drift into the arms of peace, but then I found myself struggling at the last moments to force myself to wake up and finish this damn book, that has destroyed so much of my life, in a strange hope of helping incontinent children and as it unwound, protecting hopefully a cross section of society., especially those who think, none of these things can happen to them.

Sometimes I am convinced this life had been a punishment for what I didn't do, but could have done in past lives and whenever I get depressed as memories return during copying out something, [sometimes having a retentive memory is a curse, except when relating funny experiences, that are as vivid as the sad memories] I try to run away and after a couple of days those dreams return, but in a negative way, plus I go through the experience of not being able to breathe, like the death rattle of someone dying.

Except I am wide awake, a bit like hyperventilating, because it requires yet another chapter, not just to protect incontinent children, but parents and children from all walks in life, because the corrupt perverted freaks that make the laws in this country, have laws to protect them and every nonce in this country and yes yet again have some documents from the paedophile society of Great Britain aka The Law makers, that gives freaks free access to your children with immunity…well 98% of the time.

If nothing else and I do find a way to get this on the internet, at least a few more people will understand that to postulate is to have an unproven theory that has to be accepted wholeheartedly as being self-evident and never to be questioned.

But just remember…The only people, who can or will be capable of accepting the postulations of psychology, are those who need excuses to have very conscious desires to indulge in perverted sex with their parents or children

Well not being an Authority on the Postulations of Delusions, that Have to be taken as Self-Evident, then the only conclusion can be, is that: "Insanity is caused by; 'An Innocent Person's Desire To Seek for the Truth!"

Which is something "Perfectly Normal People" will Never Do, because it may involve questioning those who have been convincing them, that they have Absolute Unquestionable Authority over them and their lives, Being Their Superiors and Equal in Wisdom only to God, but they overlook a small detail, that to make such an Unquestionable claim, puts them in A Very Questionable Situation!

Chapter 6
Conclusions

I t is now 24 years, since I started writing this book and what follows are just some of the reasons why, it has taken so long.

Now there is a bit of a problem, because none of this was put on paper or into the computer, well some of it was, but due to a series of events they became lost or stolen, by my evil daughter.

Now I am trying to sort out my memories of that period, well maybe not the memories, but the order they came about in and in some cases the back ground, plus I am 70 years old now and this has taken up too much of my life, plus things such as senior moments, whereby I compose a sentence in my mind, that vanishes as soon as I have written a few words, then add to that almost every time I fall asleep I dream of being dead.

Not that the dreams are morbid…far from it, in fact several times I have tried to hide in my dreams and fulfil a desire not to wake up, but then I remember this book and negative dreams take over, that terrify me into trying to wake up, oh they are not bedroom dreams, I can't remember the last time I slept in a bed, I stop to relax, then fall into instant sleep, sometimes when about to take a sip of a drink and wake up with the contents of the mug, it's worse with cold liquids because I think I have become incontinent again…and yes sometimes I wish I had never had the operation, especially never having to write this book and the anguish it has bought about, but then now if I have slept for a few hours, it's due to needing to use the loo, that takes a few minutes to empty my bladder and the stench makes me feel so grateful---it must be terrible for older people with incontinence, with or without incontinence wear and to think when I was a lot younger I looked forward to getting old and blame the problem on age, that is more acceptable by the public, who make excuses for you or families who try to disguise the stench.

Plus it is great when in public places and get the urge to go to the toilet, I can wait another hour or so, before it becomes like urge incontinence, even if my body is packing up on me, I get cramps in my hands and legs, I can hardly walk very far, I stumble when trying to stand up and dread falling over or sitting on the floor, because it is extremely hard to stand up again, plus all those things I enjoyed doing 2 years ago, such as long walks or doing gardening have vanished, add to that friends ten years older than myself and fitter, but having said that, just as many friends dropping dead who were younger and fitter than myself, but then my night caps have changed slightly over the years to a couple of shots of Tia Maria in my coffee, plus a couple of nearlies---roll-ups with resin or foliage in them and no roaches, which maybe the reason the government makes them illegal, they make life a lot more bearable for a lot of people, although yes it has its negative effects, such as fancying an ice-cream at 3 a.m. and the freezer is just too far to stagger to…but hey it makes life more interesting, plus not having any appetite when going through stress, it's very affordable on a pension as an ounce can last a year…plus with my hands shaking so much, they are harder to roll, so I have to eat bits with chocolate, but at least my smoking has been reduced, because when my hands shake, the roll up goes everywhere before I can lick the paper, although at times with tongue in cheek I tell my younger friends, that the worse part of shaky hands is when visiting the loo, I end up knocking a couple out before the urine pours fourth [?].

Although I wish I could remember times and dates over the last 24 years or how they came about, so I will just do the same as in much of this book, just write another letter to you with digressions thrown in…the facts will still be there but not in a chronological order.

Maybe this section should be observed by people with psychologically disturbed kids and why they should dump them as soon as it becomes obvious, that they are not sick, but just plain evil.

So this is about my evil daughter; [For Legal reasons I have to change her name, seems the laws protect evil people, so I changed it to someone in the phone book where there are dozens of Fletchers, but her first name is Nat!]

Not long after writing the original book and finding it hard to find a publisher, who said they would only be interested in a book, that includes being found innocent…although the book is about incontinence and my personal experiences caused by it, they were not interested, but then most of them published medical books, that my experiences contradicted and why wouldn't it, it's based on medical facts, as opposed to the perverted postulations of psychology.

Anyway after sending a copy to my Q.C. friend Ron Trott, who insisted I scrap the part of going to court etcetera, as it would be obvious to any legal expert that it was pure fantasy, I started trying to find the evidence.

Then one night on coming home I found my daughter reading parts of it and explained why it was hard to find a publisher and clear my name...the effect this had on her, was for her to get excited and how it would impress her friends, knowing I could not prove my case, in a law court.

The next day her mother called me to say how stupid I was to tell her, what I had done, because she was telling all her friends, when I asked why she would do it, it was pointed out she had hated me all her life...for no known reasons, in fact she seems to hate everyone...but she was always bringing her friends here for weekends and to go off on adventures...then years later that the original reasons her friends came to stay was to prevent her from beating her "friends" up, it turned out everyone was terrified of her, but when she visited me she was as nice as pie...it also turned out that they loved coming here, because they envied her for having such a great dad, who took her out so often, unlike their dads and whenever I was in the area would beg me to let them come on adventures with us...although from time to time she would arrive in tears, because her mother was always going out with her boy-friends and dumping her and her brother on baby-sitters, plus were given £1 to buy food for the weekend, that vanished almost immediately on sweets, so I told them to come home for a Sunday lunch, plus if I had no work for the Saturday they could stay all weekend and we spent a lot of holidays together...until one day Paul came to see me and said he didn't want to see me anymore, because if I went into a shop, Natasha can have anything she wants, but because he is only my godson, I wouldn't buy him something...

I became very embarrassed and tried to recall the time it had happened, in fact I was getting depressed because I would never knowingly do such a thing, then more or less begged him to tell me when it happened and to forgive me...he replied that it had never happened, but his mother had told him, it could happen and I just could not convince him it would never happen and has never happened...at that time he was 8 years old, but his mother was weird like that...a bit like when they were toddlers, if they saw me in the street, they would run up for hugs and kisses, until their stupid mother, suggested that as Paul could run faster than Natasha, I should ignore him, before hugging my daughter...so I told her where to get off, as I was the only father he had ever known and I loved him as my son.

Maybe I should explain a bit of history.

I met her [my daughter's mother] in a bar looking very sad and very pregnant and worried about going home, so I took her home safely, on the way she explained how the father of her baby dumped her, when she discovered she was pregnant and she didn't get on with her step-father, I left my bike on the seafront and walked her home to make sure she was okay, she told me when it was due I promised to visit her in hospital, which I did as he was born on Boxing Day and promised to buy some things for the baby, a week later she turned up on my doorstep with her bags, having been thrown out by her mother [who every time I saw her, was going out with someone else] anyway I let her stay for a few days to sort out her situation with the SS...now that was a big mistake, because when my girl-friend turned up whilst I was out, she informed her that we were getting married...I should have dumped her, the chances are if she hadn't the baby, I would have but couldn't bring myself to do so, as it was winter and most agencies were closed, but then the fates smiled gently on me, as her mother reported her to Social Services, who gave her the choice of living with me without her baby or keeping the baby and living in care...it turned out she chose to live with me, which didn't please me at all, then her mother reported me on some other obscure pretext, having a hatred towards her daughter, in the meantime I told her she could lose all her friends if they found out she had dumped her baby to live with someone who had just been nice to her, then she told the SS she wanted her baby back and saw legal aid, who managed to get the ruling that she could live with me during the day, but apart at night, which meant renting 2 houses, which wasn't what I could afford, so they put her in a hostel and hey I soon got over her, but seeing Paul's empty cot when I got home each night, made me very depressed and I had to avoid toyshops because the toy cars etcetera was too much for me and yeah I was pretty naïve, considering I had only been out a couple of years and still in this sort of holiday mood, where everything was still new to me...but I really did miss Paul and our morning hugs...okay he would sometimes start to cry, but I threatened to stop his pocket money, that always worked, even if he was too young to understand the concept of money and once a month would travel to Colchester to see them, taking them to the park or to Clacton forming an even greater bond between Paul and Myself.

Yet unbeknown to me she was making strange plans and getting very randy whenever we were together, well she was not unattractive...then she got pregnant and started demanding maintenance money for both the kids, then the SS informed her, that if we were to get married we could keep both children...so I went ahead and started saving my cash to get married, then I was made redundant and told her to cut back on trivia, as any extra cash would be needed for the kids, I had no idea about child benefits etcetera and she went off her head saying I thought more of the kids than I did of her and told her, I expected her to put the kids before me, then a few weeks later she informed me the wedding was off as she had met someone else...hence I didn't see her for a few years and a couple of dumped marriages... then she married Paul's father who also dumped her after a couple of months, then asked me to forgive her and to marry her...well okay I liked her a bit, but alarm bells started ringing at the idea of marrying anyone, who was dumped so often and could not keep her legs together…just like her mother and as it turned out, her grandmother as well.

Now it should be pointed out, that although I had only lived in society for less than 2 years, still under some vague observation, that wasn't obvious…by having a lot of privileges other ex-lifers were denied, but getting married to a woman with two kids, was sanctioned by the Home Office and Department of Health, but both were over-ruled by the local SS, but we kept in touch occasionally, due to that bond between me and the kids.

It would seem she inherited her personality from a long line of scrubbers and as it turned out my daughter was no different, I tried to keep out of it, but then she started demanding maintenance, that I knew was for the pubs and clubs with her latest pick-ups, but not being allowed contact with my daughter or godson…I told her not to expect a penny, but I would buy my daughters clothing, which I could only do if I knew her clothing sizes and to do that would require a day out with her, once a month visiting all the shops, then Paul started coming out with us, until we would get home to discover their mother had gone out clubbing and a neighbour told me to take them to a baby-sitter, who no one seemed to know where she lived, so I took them home and put them to bed, then about midnight the mother phoned me to say where the baby-sitter lived, but I refused to wake them up to go in search of the baby sitter.

After that I was babysitting every other weekend, which put a block on my romantic life, whilst the mother was out clubbing most nights, if she couldn't get a babysitter she just left them on their own, which I discovered when going around one night, to see about taking the kids on holiday to Stonehenge and Glastonbury, until Paul was 8 years old and refused to come out with us anymore, because his stupid mother, telling him not to complain if I got something for my daughter and not him, then he ended up getting into all sorts of trouble, wrecking the homes of anybody that let him stay overnight , because he wanted to be with his mother, in fact my daughter for the most part was a pain in the butt for the same reason, but neither of them got any affection from their mother, except if it looked as if the kids were going up for adoption, then with the threat of losing child benefits, she would be nice for a few weeks, before the hearing where the kids were promised gifts to say they wanted to stay with her, then back to her same old ways, giving the kids £1 every Friday night, to buy their own food for the entire weekends, hence Paul came back into my life for decent meals and our annual trips to Glastonbury and the Lord Mayors Show, but then after a couple of years they started arguing and fighting all the time…so Paul stopped visiting…it took a long time to realise it was my evil daughter causing all the problems and how she would violently attack other kids in her area, having caught her a few times beating up smaller kids, especially [Karen Small who was a great little girl, always polite and chatty] then when I asked my evil daughter why she was so nasty to the local kids, she would just say; whenever she was upset, she just had to hurt someone, plus her mother told me she would spend hours in front of the mirror practicing crying, hence I stopped her from coming around for a few months, then everyone started telling me to dump her as she was evil, a compulsive liar and would destroy my life. But just like all those other parents with disturbed kids, I thought I could help her…well I had helped a lot of other kids and adults get through periods of depressions, so why not her?

Plus I had completely overlooked the difference, between psychologically disturbed kids and outright evil monsters, the former can't help it, whereas the evil freaks made it a life-time ambition, to enjoy destroying people's lives.

It may sound weird, but I am sure there must be millions just like me, who are connected by the strange blood bond, like a lot of mother's will always forgive their sons, regardless to how violent they are towards their mothers who are eagerly awaiting the day they will change and it's the same with daughters, that are constantly on the point of maturity, respecting themselves and the lives of people around them, plus I have no idea how many times I tried to convince her that the easiest thing in life to lose is respect…that may… but usually will never be regained and the only experience of it will be from strangers that respect each other initially…my problem was my constantly forgetting what a brilliant actress she could be, adding to that what a convincing liar as well and it took a few more years, to just give up, move out of the area and ask people I met, not to tell her.

Oh I may as well bung it in now, in case I forget later; one night she sent me a text, asking if I still love her…well in the past this question usually preceded a request for a babysitter or an "urgent" loan, so I replied Why? She went ballistic… but note she didn't speak to me direct but sent me another message, saying if I loved her I would say so…Yes or No!

She then repeated her question, to which I replied; Well as much as any father would his child or any mother would her children…adding well about as much as she loves Lorien…it was a simple as that, but still didn't improve the lives of her children and had already been banned by the SS on her request to prevent me seeing my grandchildren.

We have not communicated in years and had I realised this when she was 10 years old…I may have had a much happier life…so take note all you devoted fathers of monsters, that look as human as everyone else, either dump them or do the world a favour and make them disappear for eternity.

Wow that was some digression, but back to the preceding history…

…so I started taking her out again, but always with a couple of her friends, to keep her occupied if I needed a rest or was in agony from my stomach ulcers [but pretending I was okay, so as not to spoil their day out] that doctors kept refusing to treat, as they amongst all my other incontinence problems were brushed aside as being all in my mind, which in part was why I rarely saw doctors, because unlike everyone else, without bladder problems, all my physical problems were all in my mind and treatment usually came when threatening them…oh I was into weight training and lots of running and Chairman Mao's 5 minute exercises…hence using a bit of psychology against them , even though I was strong physically I would run a mile to avoid confrontation…and it took years to figure out which foods caused the most pains---mainly onion's.

I was having terrible bile attacks in Broadmoor, but like everything else, if I did not help them via an act of self-incrimination, they weren't prepared to offer me help, but then I was sent there for acting strangely after being refused dental treatment for years, for not playing ball with them, but most of the inmates thinking they were doing me a favour, gave me lots of painkillers that eventually caused my stomach ulcers, but a month before going to Broadmoor, the prison called in a mobile dental surgery and removed half or more of my teeth, hence by the time I got to Broadmoor, I was acting almost normal again.

But back to taking out her friends as a distraction, when I needed to rest, plus it had a good side effect in so far as she discovered every one of her friends envied her for having such a great father, as their fathers never took them anywhere and whenever I was in the area, they would beg me to let them come on our next day out…we never really had a limit if we were going to the beach or countryside to explore or climb trees…then it depended on how many could squeeze into the back of my transit, after taking everything out of it and before setting out everyone had to help prepare a big picnic…but it only changed when going to London she could take 3 friends who were all charged £3 each, towards the train fare, ice-creams, plus the extra food…they came here the night before that gave us a better day out, starting early instead of visiting their homes to pick them up, either still in bed or taking hours to get dressed and losing half the day, although much as I liked little Karen, her turning up at the station, then claiming she had lost her money only worked twice, after that I would collect her money from her mother, oh yeah it sounds like a cheap day out, but if they came up with the £3 I would then give them the same amount on top, but then I did have a family rail card, that allowed me to take up to 4 kids for £1 each, we discovered all the free museums and those perpetual South Bank fairs, put on by Ken Livingstone when he was in charge of the GLC and usually it was on the last train home…another advantage of staying for the weekend, this went on for a few years before discovering my daughter was taking bribes from the other kids for our days out.

Plus they loved playing board games and Scrabble, Which I kept cheating at, not to win but to get them to challenge easy words , but on field trips we would take illustrated nature books , where they had to read out the descriptions as I pretended to study the plants…they never realised until they were much older, that each day out was an educational trip but also great fun…which is the way education should be taught, but then I made a very bad error…I taught them how to banter and what great fun they could have using logic…okay this upset a lot of the parents when telling their kids to do things, they would reply; Now if you think about it logically, you would know it is impossible, for a child to know what you are speaking about!" It was my daughter's mother who enlightened the other parents that their kids were mimicking me.

Oh yes one I had one other rule with the kids [correction two rules, the other being that when final decisions were required, my word was final] and that being if they are talking about natural things, to talk about them naturally…none of that you'll know when you grow up, which is usually was told to them by their parents, by their parents for countless generations, that all grew up none the wiser, hence most did well in school, except my daughter made friends with a few no hopers and started bunking school, except for the games we had played, always got her good exam results, even if she wasn't there much…this discovery was made when I turned up at the school one day to see if my daughter could have a day off…that they Nat and Paul were always given in the primary school, whenever an historical event was taking place, so instead of in years to come they don't lament they were not very far away on that day, but used the day as a stepping stone through life…but it turned out, no one knew where she was, she would arrive at school, sign in and then disappear for the rest of the day and had been doing for a long time.

By the time she was 11 years old, things started going missing in the house, then one day having to return home for some chemicals for a job and I discovered she had broken into the house, gone through most of my draws and was sat reading it, I told her I didn't want her breaking in [mainly due to any chemicals left lying around…they were usually under lock and key, when the kids were here] to the house and to let me know when she was off school.

Anyway she asked about the book, having read most of it [that was how it originally was, before proving a point…it may appear as Book One] so I explained how I was trying to find a publisher and most didn't want to know unless I managed to get an appeal and win, not that the book was based on the trial, but predominantly on what life had been like growing up with incontinence.

Then pointed out the reality that it is easier to prove what you have done, but not be able to prove what you haven't done or proving a negative, using the example; that it is easier for a man to prove he is married, than it is for a man to prove he is not married.

Later that night after she had gone home, her mother phoned me to ask why I had told her my history, so I explained what had happened, to which she replied, my daughter was going around telling all her friends I am a nonce case, when I said that was hard to believe, plus asking her why she would want to do such a thing… it seems my daughter had hated me all her life for no known reason, in fact she hated everyone in her family, well I could understand why she hated her mother, but not me and her brother and sister.

Of course it back fired on her and she lost a few friends, when she started telling all her friends, who knew what a nonce was, because they had spent several weekends here, plus I had baby sat with a lot of their friends and okay when they got really dirty on our trips, falling into mud or climbing moss covered trees, I put them all in the bath, washed their clothes, plus if they were ill at school and their parents were out, they would come to me [if I was at home] and I would look after them as if they were my own children, plus if they wanted to stay overnight for our weekend adventures, I would check first with their parents…none of that well their mums said it was okay or giving me a note, plus I would give the parents a business card, just in case they needed to contact me about their kids.

I didn't see my daughter again for a couple of years, because she was put into foster care, with a really nice family on Canvey Island, who took her to the theatre a lot and holidays, plus I had been trying for years to have her with me, but each time we went to the children's court, she would come out with some crap, on the spur of the moment and I would just freeze, as I tried to recall the non-event , which made me look very guilty of her convincing fantasy…for which her mother rewarded her with treats and cigarettes , hence I thought it odd that should go into care.

Her mother told me that she had gone into school one day crying so convincingly that after the teachers and school nurse, managed to calm her down, she told them that whenever she stayed with me, I kept trying to get into bed with her…the truth being she kept trying to get into my, bed, but because she would fidget so much, I sent her back to her room complaining I didn't love her anymore, but then it turned out she had a few friends in care, who were genuine victims of incest… hence no one questioned me, because she was such a convincing actress and liar, but after a couple of years she walked out on her foster carers on the grounds they were very selfish, in so far as they let their own daughter chose her birthday and Xmas presents, but she only got what they wanted to give her...which were very nice gifts anyway.

Yet I leap forward too far, going back to the book and explaining why I could not find a publisher, after contacting so many publishing companies, that included Ron Trott who told me to remove the bit about the trial bit, as it was obvious to anyone in a legal position, that it is pure fantasy, hence another three or four years seeking for proof it had taken place et etcetera.

I came home one day to find she had broken in yet again, though the louver window, by slipping out the glass and then replacing it before leaving; she took my typed list of all the quotes by incontinence experts [legal paedophiles, i.e. people who either condone it , promote it or justify paedophilia and who's to say indulge in it, against incontinence children], plus a few chapters from my book and some copies of letters from Ron...that resulted in a visit one evening from a couple of Home Office Officials, threatening to have me returned to Broadmoor for violating my condition for discharge...i.e. if I ever found the evidence to prove my innocence and tried to take it to a court of appeal, it would be seen as a relapse of any imaginary isms they would come up with, sadly enough I should have done one of two things, neither of which I did, one let them lock me away again, because all those Human Rights societies, only help those still in prison [publicity] or adopted the theory that I had become a psychopath and a schizophrenic and killed my evil daughter...well at least it would have been a novelty to actually be guilty of a crime...oddly enough although it was claimed in court that being incontinent at 17 makes me a psychopath and liable to become schizophrenic , my daughter is not incontinent, but definitely a schizophrenic .

When I confronted her about the visit from the Home Office and informing them I was planning to take my evidence to the Court of Appeal, she just laughed, pointing out that until my name was cleared, I wouldn't be able to prove a negative and anyway it did not matter what she did, I always gave her another chance... which sadly was true, plus it helped her justify hurting me, instead of her friends who never forgave her needless to say, I yet again banned her from my home, then when she appeared to have matured mentally, gave her yet another chance.

Anyway there are more ways of killing a cat than by skinning it...plus not wanting to go through the experiences, that led up to being persuaded to incriminate myself in whatever the authorities needed a patsy to protect one of their own... neither did I consent nor did they demand that I could not tell the World my story, plus who would have thought all those years ago, that such a thing as the world wide web, ever coming about, except in science fiction stories, a bit like how I managed to prove the trial took place, by watching the film 1984!

Then my computer started going wrong, with a strange number appearing at the top of the screen, so I took it along to Estuary Computers in Southend, who decided they did not know what it meant, but decided that as it took too long to start up, they would speed it up my computer. As it turned out [too late] to be a code to warn me that it was overheating, hence the result being the computer burnt itself out, but fortunately much of the book was on floppy disk, but then it took many more years before I found out how to go about getting on modern media.

At about this time another curse entered my life in the form of Dr P M Lafferty and is still at the Queensway Clinic, but no longer my GP, when he introduced himself, he pointed out that he had seen in my medical notes that I have severe incontinence, to which I pointed out was ancient history, that had been solved years ago, plus it must have taken him 30 seconds to read my notes, that were only 2-3 pages long as I rarely ever saw a doctor, hence being passed on from doctor to doctor… so much for the No Hope Service.

Not only did he put me down to see another urologist miles away in Orsett, but he put me on the list for a third operation, as if GP's have a far greater knowledge than a qualified surgeon, anyway I sent them a not very polite letter, suggesting what they can do with both their hospital and urologist, then made an appointment with Lafferty again, because I was in quite a bit of pain because of their quackery, hence he gave me some medication pills, called Uripas to be taken three times a day, then told me which chemist stocked them, pointing out they have no side-effects whatsoever, when I collected them, they did not contain any warnings or those bits of paper that cover any form of side effects, nor anything else come to that…

Well it's not that I am paranoid in general, but from too many previous experiences with the NHS, decided to take one a day, then if they seemed okay, I would increase the dose.

After a few days I started feeling drowsy, but after a bit of self-analysis, put it down to the extra contract in North Essex, hence I was leaving at 5 p.m. and getting home about 6 a.m.

Then after a few more days, I stopped to let a car out of a side turning, then slowly went ahead and blacked out, hit the bus stop sign, but fortunately going so slowly, I did not hit the queue of people waiting on the other side, hence getting my mate to take the van home and stormed off to see Lafferty, who swore blind he had told me not to drive or use machinery, then during the argument, he implied that maybe I was becoming senile…I was just coming up to my 50th birthday, but he insisted it was not unusual for it to hit younger people, so my employee started doing all the driving, but things started getting very bad, especially as I was using some very corrosive chemicals on some of the jobs, plus forgetting to do things, but for some odd reason I didn't stop the one a day pill, but fortunately never increased the dosage.

In the end I handed over the work and took some time off, because I was forgetting too many things…

Then one day whilst stood in my kitchen making a cuppa, I heard a lot of hooting outside, so I stepped outside to see what was happening, only to discover I was a mile away, in the middle of the main road during the rush hour, with absolutely no idea how I got there, then wandered off to see a friend, who thought I was stoned, on the one hand I wasn't and on the other had given up using acid a few years before hand due to its inferior quality, then something [in retrospect] great happened, I again found I had no idea where I was, but looking around saw another friend's house, so I knocked on the door, pointing out I was just passing and decided to say hello, his reply being I had just left this house, plus I had been there several hours and won all their money at a card game they had just introduced me to, but then the Fates smiled gently on me, because his girl-friend was a state registered nurse, who asked me if I were on any medication, then took me to the reference library to check out prescribed medication.

It implied the medication had no known side effects, but made reference to another drug it had once been known as, but it had been banned around the world except in Britain, where its name had been changed and just by luck, the library had the previous version of Mimms, now that was an eye-opener as it had 17 side effects of which 8 could prove fatal, bloody typical of this country to change its name, after too many people were dying, but another great side effect being it caused forgetfulness, so I had been forgetting to take it on a regular basis.

Now had I been married or living with a devoted partner, who like most women make sure the husbands followed the prescribed dosages, I should have been dead within a couple of weeks, considering it was a course of involuntary euthanasia tablets…probably designed to eradicate people who were suffering from incontinence and therefore psychopaths with schizophrenic tendencies!

I was then given a sickness note for 28 days…which being self-employed isn't easy, then told by the job centre, to take it to the DHS, who in return told me to report to them after 28 days, this I did, but the 28th day would have been on a Sunday, I queried if I should take it to them on the Friday or the Monday, they replied that I need not get another certificate for a year, when I pointed out I needed to get back to work, they replied I will never work again, then asked them to explain why and they just referred me to my GP, that turned out to be upset for refusing to have an operation, I did not need…well I don't consider myself to be unique, plus the ease in which it was done, makes me wonder just how many people's lives have been destroyed or apparently been murdered, with immunity from anyone being able to have them investigated, by anyone after taking 21 pills a week, instead of 7 pills… as I took and almost died, I contacted the BMA who replied that unless the GP admits he made an error, when it became clear it was deliberate…so it would seem until the NO HOPE SERVICE is destroyed, these overpaid freaks are guaranteed a job for life.

Plus during the time of all my confusion, I lost almost everything, some shares, my pension policies and an account set aside for periods of sickness…but then that's the price everyone pays who banked with NatWest.

Needless to say it was several years before I saw Lafferty again and from the look on his face, he must have thought he was seeing my ghost, although I had complained to the useless British Medical Association, who just kept repeating I should get him to sign a statement admitting error, but to get such a letter would have required the sun to rise in the west, proving he is the Son of God, plus it would have been interesting to know how many of his patients he had caused the deaths of, considering the ease in which he tried to kill me…unaware that I had long since given up almost all hope or trust in GP's after years of their contempt towards people with severe incontinence .

So I spent the last of my money on a boat, gave up on all doctors and it took a further 8 years to recover from the side effects!

Sorry this is becoming very confusing as much of it has already been covered, so I will just cover my Evil Daughter.

*   *   *   *   *

Yeah okay, a lot of my problems were caused by giving her "Just One More Chance" just like so many other parents…many of whom ended up being murdered by their kids for no apparent reasons, except maybe saying; "Enough is Enough!" and then saying "No" to their final demands.

Then one day she turned up at the house, she was about 15 years old at the time, saying her mother was concerned about not seeing me for some time, but as per usual, it was some completely different reason…

Now if you are fortunate enough, never having to be the parents of one of those evil freaks, you will never understand, how happy a parent feels, when convinced they have grown out of being so bloody evil, plus our relationship on good days were great and most of her life, we had bantered together and yeah maybe I was too laid back most of the time, but then much of the mirth was to override my sorrows that hovered just behind my façade, so anything funny was welcomed…

Hence when she asked me, what would happen if she were to have a baby, what would I do?

Well thinking it was a rhetorical question, I replied, well for starters I would become a granddad and visit the park more often, to which she replied; she was pregnant, but instead of hitting the roof, plus not having thought the answer out, I replied; "Oh Thanks for breaking it to me gently!"

But she refused to say who the father was, then added insult to injury, pointed out she had no idea, but just hoped it looked like the father, so she could claim maintenance from him, yep just like her mother's ideas of perfect boyfriends, discuss marriage after going out of her way to get pregnant, then at the eleventh hour call it all off, due to having found someone else, but the fathers had to pay just the same…

At this point I should have dumped her, but instead I started making plans to help her out, well I could hardly thrust my hand and pull it out, then off she went home, but it was several months before I saw her again, but then it was only because her mother told me she was about to get married and neither her mother or myself were invited to the wedding…it turned out she had moved in with the freak who only preferred school girls [which I only found out a couple of years later, when she moved out] he was keeping all the local girls in fags and booze, then raping her drunken friends, only to become very sorry, pointing out it was caused by being too drunk to prevent it, they all fell for it, plus it would be best if they did not tell anyone, because all their friends would call them slags and they fell for it…seems he had a reputation for deflowering young teenagers, but then on the estate where he lived were a lot of paedophiles, with a couple of guys meeting up in prison for raping their own kids, unaware of which each other had been up to, until meeting in nick, plus living next door to each other.

Anyway I went to see her and sure enough they were getting married and was told that being her father I had to pay for her wedding dress and put on a dinner, so I pointed out that if they thought, I was going to pay for a wedding I was not invited to and it had already been arranged that someone else would give her away… she must be living on another planet.

A few weeks later she decided she would be inviting all her family [but then only in the hope they buy her good gifts] after al…well having just invested in some heavy duty cleaning equipment, I offered to fill her freezer, leading up to the date, but if she wanted a wedding dress to go to a charity shop, but I would buy the wedding cake [ha ha].

Plus I met his terrified kids, who were about to become step-grandchildren, they never laughed or were cautious about smiling, the girl was 11 years old, but like her brother did not have any friends, because as soon as they started making friends, they would get home from school where their bags were packed and he would suddenly move…probably to escape from his victims, it seems they had lived at 9 addresses by the time she had reach 11 years old, but hey I really do enjoy taking kids out on adventures, with picnics…and what a job I had trying to get them to smile, longer to reassure them they could laugh out loud.

Then one night when I called in to see my daughter, he started asking me about my trial, as my daughter had told him everything, but slightly twisted to suit her own evil, so I showed him the forensic reports and police statements, hence he had no fears of me taking them out, either together or separately, they would stay weekends on my boat or on trips to London [staying overnight with me] and took them with me camping with the blind, plus by the time we visited Woodlarks in Surrey, they were just like any other kids and when not playing with the other kids, they excelled in communicating with the deaf/blind and became their sighted guides, then one night I heard Martin crying in his sleep, but instead of waking him, I listened to him crying; "I am tall enough…I am tall enough!"

We had been to Chessington World of Adventure, but he was too small for most of the rides, but I still wish I had been carrying a camera the following year, when he walked tentatively to the bar and the sheer look of joy on his face, when he realized how much he had grown…was priceless.

Plus during those 2 years, they had made loads of friends and were full of confidence, so much so that when Emma was 13 and budding out, she ran away from home to live with her grandmother, after he started checking her [with his hands] her breast and vagina, then after seeking my advice, ran off to her grans, with her father telling everyone, he had thrown her out for being a liar.

*   *   *   *   *

Oh I forgot a bit…before I discovered his lust for school girls, the night before the original date for the wedding, my daughter had her hen party, that ended up with all her cousins and ex-boy-friends having a gang bang, on the grounds it would be their last chance, then went home completely drunk and told him all about it, so the wedding was called off, then a week later it was back on again.

But back to my daughter…over the same period, Lorien had been born, no one had told me, but I had hitherto convinced myself it was going to be a boy, then early one morning in the middle of November, I was coming out of a night club when the notion, that Lorien was about to be born and stopped halfway down the stairs, I had never in my wildest dreams, imagined the baby to be anything other than a boy, hence I called the maternity unit to discover my daughter was in labour, then visiting her an hour after she was born.

Now an odd thing about my daughter conceiving, was for some unknown reason, I was getting morning sickness, no idea why especially as none of them were down to me…then when Joshua was conceived, I asked if she were pregnant again, she said no, then a few days later discovered she "WAS" pregnant again, then working it out backwards, it appeared I became aware of it almost on the point of conception.

Any way back to Lo [Lorien] the parents told everyone how stupid I had become, having spent one and a half hours, talking to a newly born baby and refused to listen, when I pointed out that I was not talking to her so much as communicating with her along the lines from Little Red Riding Hood, saying things like, "Oh Lorien what nice eyes you have!" followed by saying; "All the better to see the flowers with granddad"…then onto her nose to smell the flowers, then what a nice mouth…all the better to tell you how much I love you Granddad!"

I was constantly popping in to say hello to her, taking her for walks in her pram or shopping for clothing.

When she was about three weeks old, it seems when Martin opened the front door and called out it was Granddad, Lorien rolled over and looked towards the door, at which her idiot parents said it was merely a coincidence, because according to the experts, young babies can't recognise anyone, especially not names…then it became a tussle between Martin and myself, who would hold her, so I pointed out he could see her all day and I for a few hours and each time I held her I chatted continuously…she was very special…but then most grandparents will say that, except her other grandparents didn't give a damn and rarely walked the hundred yards from around the corner, but then they refused to communicate with our daughter, when she was born and she all but grew up with baby-sitters or myself.

Then people started pointing out the strange relationship we had, after taking her shopping one day for clothing, that on getting home proved to be the right size and yes I have a lousy history of buying clothing for kids…which was part of the reason I used to take her out shopping when Lo's mother was a kid, I used it as an excuse to spend more time with her…hence when my daughter asked how I knew what to buy, I pointed our Lo had chosen them, this caused my daughter to come out shopping with us, with me pointing out a frown meant No and a smile meant Yes…then an old lady came over and pointed out, if she hadn't seen it with her own eyes, she would have said it was impossible for us to communicate, it was almost as if she were a special gift and yep I all but adored her and she me.

Then whenever I had done her parents a favour and asked what I would be charging, I just said I would like to take her out for a few hours and often shared those hours with Martin.

Then I didn't see her for a while, having a lot of work coming in, so the next time I saw her briefly, was a few days before the wedding, delivering enough food to fill her freezer on a budget wedding party [which needless to say was all eaten, before the wedding, but maybe their contempt tasted really good].

Then on the big day as with most family occasions, everyone had to hold the baby, passing it rapidly on to the next unsuspecting person, as if it carried the plague…I was a bit late getting there as I had gone out for some booze, so by the time I got there, poor little Lo was screaming and struggling to get away from everyone, so I held her gently in my arms and started saying; "But Lorien what nice eyes you have…" she immediately stopped struggling and crying, her eyes popped wide open and she threw her arms around my neck and refused to let go…which she only did after she fell into a deep sleep.

Then her greedy mother demanded to know where the wedding cake was, so I walked back to my van and returned with a very large box, that I took down the garden, telling everyone to stand well back, then produced a massive multi-shot display firework [that at the time, were not on sale to the public, but I had some connections, especially when my friends saw my joke] and anyway why buy a cake covered in marzipan, I hate the stuff and every wedding I had been too, implied everyone else hates it, with my daughter walking around moaning, She should have known better, than to trust me to buy a cake! No idea why because I was always buying or making cakes, that I refuse to eat on my birthday, then can justify 364 cakes as compensation.

Okay to give the guy some credit, after she walked out on him, apparently for the same reason she married him…for consuming too much booze, plus the fact she had Lorien, she would go to him for favours, then got pregnant again, it turned out to be his kid and they were still having sex on the grounds she wasn't getting it anywhere else, until she told me she fancied going to night school to improve her chances of getting work…and yes muggings fell for it, so I ended up babysitting a few nights a week, whilst she attended college.

But hey I was distracted to the fact she was getting dressed up to the nines, just to go to college, plus Josh would scream for hours on end and nothing I did would calm him, very much unlike Lo, then one night in utter frustration almost to the point of snapping, I put him in his cot…turned to leave the room and he suddenly stopped screaming and went deadly quiet…and did I panic, so much so that I called for an ambulance, repeatedly pointing out I had not hit him or violently shaken him [there were a lot of cases in the courts at the time of babies being shaken to death] but it turned out it wasn't unusual for babies to just stop screaming, but hey very scary to the uninformed.

A few days later I took the kids to the park and Lo pointed to a wine bar, saying it was mummies college, she was very insistent, so we carried on to the park near the college and popped in for a prospectus, thinking it would be a good idea to brush up on 9 volt power…living on a boat, then glancing through it, discovered the whole building was closed at 8 p.m. hence asking about those classes that ended at 10 pm., having been repeatedly told by her they closed at 10 p.m. and the tutor would invite them all back for coffee and sometimes the time flew by, that was the reason why some nights she wouldn't get back until well past midnight.

It also took some weeks to realise she never took any note books or never returned home with any homework, but then I was distracted by Lo, when her mother was getting ready to go out, plus it was not unusual for me and Lo to travel quite a distance, before saying to her; "I think we have forgotten something!" Then she would reply; "Sorry Granddad" and we would have our greeting cuddle and kiss… okay we were both guilty of it, but unlike her mother at that age, she never demanded money or sweets in return for affection, maybe that's why she always froze when I gave her a hug, just like with Lo's grandmother.

But with Lo it was special, we just loved being together and most of the time words were not needed, plus her love was obvious, because everywhere we went, she would tell everyone I was her Granddad and the other reason my daughter managed to con me, was apparently down to her great act of having become more mature and a better mother than she had, had.

Then it reached the point that compulsive liars always cross over,…thinking they are so clever and taking too much for granted, by pointing out to one of my mates, how she was studying several nights a week, the same subjects he was on, this resulted in her having to pay for a babysitter for some months afterwards, although on occasions I was really feeling down, I would turn up to take Lo out and she would always be ready, having told everybody I was coming around to take her out, usually hours before the notion crossed my mind and it was just by chance I was in the area.

A year after Lo was born and her mother deciding it would be great to be a single mother [convinced as with most of her negative choices, via the latest story line in a soap opera], we were walking home one night when she suddenly slapped Lo for no apparent reason, then when asking why she had hit her, it turned out her mother decided she hated her, because none of her dubious friends liked Lo, which was hard to accept, because all my friends loved her and everywhere we went people loved her…but it turned out it seemed Lo was the reason she couldn't go out clubbing every night, so I suggested she got different friends…but she was a typical scrounger, never had a job or earned any money etcetera…so I pointed out that was the joys of being a single parent, spending lots of quality time with her children , as she got herself pregnant time after time, then I offered to babysit for a few hours, knowing loads of single parents would appreciate a couple of hours with old friends, in exchange for a meal.

I turned up at 8 pm. and off she went for four hours, whilst me and the kids went to Adventure Island…until closing time…they never ran out of energy…then 10 hours later she turned up with the last misfit off the seafront, went straight into her bedroom, without asking how I or the kids were, then moaned when the kids woke her up for some breakfast…when Josh arrived she hated him even more, then I pointed out to Lo's mum that 4 hours was more than enough time considering I had to work the next day…she turned up 12 hours later and accused me of being selfish and if it hadn't been for the bond between me and Lo…I should have dumped her there and then.

Then one night the guy she had picked up from the seafront [who turned out to be a very nice guy, like so many of the others] phoned to say she had gone off in a rant and told him to keep the kids, because he obviously loved them more than he did her [she doesn't like to share her pick-ups with anyone], when I got there the police were there, asked who I was and left it at that…they should have had her put on a mental health section, for everyone's sake.

After a few weeks, she came out with the story that social services had arranged for a family to look after her kids for a week to give her a break…well unlike her I don't make a habit of steaming open private correspondence …living on a boat I needed a postal address, but lying on the table in full view of everyone was a letter about adoption, then she pointed out how much better off the kids would be… quoting yet another plot from a soap opera, about how having kids so young would destroy her teen years…

Well as she was such a convincing and compulsive liar and her reasons for walking out on her husband changed more often than her underwear…I went to see the guy, well it was his son she was putting up for adoption and he got an intervention, via having an affair with his the kids social worker…probably as it turned out, the only mature woman he kept serviced from time to time and got the kids, coupled with my going to see them every Friday to share a meal and read the kids bedtime stories, having a shower and a bit of a chin wag, plus taking them out, but their mother refused to go to see them, until one day the kids started crying to their teacher that they did not want to go home, because as with his own kids, he turned out to be a control freak and were sent back to live with their mother…

Sorry I am rambling…but before that had occurred I had been banned from seeing the kids on the grounds I was a backstabber, which turned out to be due to meeting the kids mother, who had moved into a flat below a friend of mine and she had another kid [Ryan] a great little guy, with whom I hit it off the moment we met…so the freak created a law whereby if I wanted to carry on seeing Lo and Josh, I had to ignore Ryan, because it meant seeing his mother, regardless of the fact I never went to see her , but obviously being Ryan's mother she was always with him…so ended up only being able to see Ryan, when his mother had all the kids, Lo's weekends on the boat got stopped, the schoolgirl stay with him got raped… apparently when he was yet again apparently drunk, but managed to terrify her into keeping quiet.

Hence the only time I got to see the kids at their mother's flat…a sort of compulsory thing, where social services had threatened to take Ryan away, if she did not let them stay with her once a fortnight…then every time I saw Lo, she ignored me and the reason took a lot of prising out of her…

Apparently the freak had given to her, for my not visiting her or Josh, was because I hated them so much and never wanted to then again…yeah I went ballistic, told the kids to put their shoes and coats and took them to my boat for fun and a picnic…then tried to convince them that I would never stop loving them and they will always be welcomed to stay with me on my boat.

Note for the previous 10 years she had stayed on my boat every other weekend, telling all the seawall walkers, her name is Lorien and she is staying on her granddads boat, then introduce them to the dogs…Jesus, Naimles and Solstice, oh and Hobbit the cat…which in return acquired a lot of passing friends who were asking if she were visiting that weekend and she was allowed to wander quite a big distance, as long as she had the dogs with her, knowing that as they would not let me, playfully have a funny fight with her…anyway the poor kids ended up with her again, then I got a phone call one night asking for £20 to buy some food for the kids… but instead of giving her cash, I went to Tesco's and spent £50 on all the things the kids had always liked, including fresh fruit and vegetables and boy did that cause her to go into a rage, because it was kids food, but then her mother turned up with some bags of food and like me got slagged off…the whilst Lynn was taking the flack, I decided to put the food in the freezer and cupboards, that were already chocker block full of food, that Vineyards [a local charity had given her]…seems she just wanted money and sod the kids. With her favourite old moan that I loved the kids more than I did her, thus she started hating the kids with a vengeance, except when we started having days out again, but she never put her hand in her purse, on the grounds that when she was small she had never paid for anything and she is still my kid…then would fly into another rage when I said okay, I will pay for her and she could pay for her kids, it got worse on a picnic if there was an extra cake and that was rewarded on the one potato, two potato rhyme…because she had always had the last cake, when she was small…overlooking she was always bragging that with 3 kids…a lot more than I had in my pockets after all my bills had been paid…until the doctor tried repeatedly and obviously unsuccessfully kept trying to kill me.

Well living on a damp boat, I decided to sort out a couple of photo albums, one each for her and Paul, plus a portfolio of every note and knickknack from throughout their lives…a month later she asked if I had any negatives, due to having destroyed all the photos that made her look fat during her childhood, when wearing bulky jumpers in the winter…vanity? In some she was only 5 years old!

Then the evil bitch dropped a bomb shell, she had got the social services, to put a ban on my seeing the kids, because I have a strange power over young children, because everywhere we went or vising her friends…usually giving her a lift… all her kids liked me for no apparent reason or when visiting a park, toddlers would bring me their books to read them a story, but at the same time most kids were terrified of her, so would just keep out of her way or politely acknowledge her presence…well it's hardly my fault that adults as well as kids, accept I am not a threat to them.

Plus I power up the imagination of kids, when playing games invented on the spur of the moment…okay it sometimes worried the parents, like when I was doing some garden work for a market trader and it started raining very heavily, so I sought cover in an old stable where loads of kids were bored, but there were a lot of foam mattresses, a rubber dingy and an old purple blanket… well what a temptation, all the kids got into the boat on top of all the foam mattresses, then I threw the blanket over them, as they went sailing the sea during the night, with tiny holes that became stars and rapidly switching the light on and off we had lightening, then the sea got choppy and the lightning flashed and in no time we were having a very violent storm and all the kids were soon screaming in terror, that in turn cause all the parents to come out in the pouring rain…shouting out "What's going on?" to which the kids screamed; "Run away or you will be drowned!"

That in part not only got me more work, but also loads of invites to children's parties or has un-birthday parties at my house…the most popular being just before Xmas when the parents could do the last of their shopping and hiding gifts away from prying little eyes…I seem to have been blessed with an ability to communicate with kids and in serious discussions, my language broke down to their own level, plus I would tell them, that if they did not understand a word, to interrupt and ask what it means, instead of ignoring them or say you will know when you grow up...

There is one thing I have never figured out and that is, how any freaks can want to rape kids or why the laws in this country, offer such freaks more protection than is on offer to other kids, okay I admit I don't like evil kids, but sometimes the barriers in their minds can be broken...maybe it's due to my own childhood and my theory brought about by Social Services not long after being discharged, that although they had no objections to me getting married and having kids, I would not be able to live with them in the same house after it gets dark [maybe they thought I was Jekyll and Hyde] on the grounds...that not having grown up in a family, I wouldn't know how to be a parent...more jewish psychology crap...is it any wonder that anyone with half a brain becomes a psychologist...this country is full of people who grew up in children's homes or with violent parents, a bit like every time a freak starves or batters their kids to death, the SS bends over backwards to protect them in court, by saying; "Well they were battered as kids, hence it is only natural for them to kill their own kids.

Whereas I adopted the idea...initially practiced on my niece Natasha, that as I did not have an uncle as a kid to take me out etcetera, then why not be for her the great uncle, I wish I had, then I became the father I wished I had and so on, the only thing those SS freaks cannot or point-blankly refuse to figure out, is why anyone would want to rape or violently beat up on defenceless kids, maybe the most important qualification needed to become such a freak/good social worker, is to have been a willing victim of incest or in their case, were privileged to have had their subconscious desires, to rape their very sick parents.

Anyway my daughter wasn't getting anywhere, with my problem of being liked by friends and their kids or loved by my grandchildren, so she decided she was still having nightmares, about the time she dreamed I wanted to rape her...well bugger me, how can I be held responsible for her sick fantasies, apart from repeatedly, when she dressed up for pulling guys how she looked, which always got the same reply; "From the neck down, she was a great turn on, but including her head she was still my daughter!"

Oh when she was 16 she discovered one of her friends had been a victim of incest and her mother wasn't charging her any rent after she left school...so she went to see the mother, practicing her tears and strange story on the way, as she begged them to let her stay with them, due to all her very realistic nightmares...

Oh dear what a mistake...of all the people who may have fallen for her charade she had chosen the family of someone, I had just spent two years convincing the girl, that not all men were rapist, less still with their own daughters…they almost beat her up and threw her out…which resulted in two things, the dirty slag started following the poor girl around until she saw her talking to guys her own age, then in a loud voice to draw everyone's attention, my evil daughter, would tell them they are wasting their time with her, because she only has sex with men that are old enough to be her father, then when she got home, thinking I was unaware of the situation, I threw her out of the house, mainly for starting rumours that I was raping her and okay partly because of the evil in which she treated the poor girl, who had been coming to my home with my daughter, until she eventually started coming on her own, then one night discovered my armchair was also a comfortable bed, then she put on an act of pretending to falling asleep, that backfired when she did fall asleep. Then several hours later, woke up repeatedly telling me how sorry she was, to which I just laughed in a nice way, pointing out she was now cured, having felt enough trust in a man without fear of falling asleep.

Oh the poor kid had been a double victim, which resulted in me discovering her history, even though previously I was aware of a deep sorrow within her and she couldn't figure out who had told me and couldn't accept I just felt it when near her…eventually I asked her mum, who was a friends sister and also how she always became very withdrawn and almost suicidal after having to visit a child councillor, who would repeatedly tell her to tell him her story, in every minute detail…that in turn cause her to become severely depressed and attempting suicide…they claim that if they remember all the details, it would make it easier to forget what happened…it's long pass the time to round up all those overpaid freaks and gas them like any other vermin!

Oh whenever I help any of those people…I always insisted that they did not give me any details of what happened, because I have bad dreams of my own, therefore didn't want any extra, oh it started with a friend telling me of his vivid dreams and now 40 years later, the dream returns to me, all they need to know is how to be treated the same as everyone else and at times when they try to convince me they were going to kill themselves, I would [tongue in cheek]offer to help them do it and pointing out how it will have so many negative results for me and being sent to prison…it usually does the trick, when they think someone would risk everything, just to bring them peace of mind and the next stage is to get them to laugh at themselves, by telling them just a little of my own history and how all the tried and tested theories on how to commit suicide, had never worked for me…

But I digress

Sometimes I think if I had never been set up in court by a highly respected sexual pervert, I would never have met those freaks that enjoyed raping and murdering kids. That in Broadmoor during therapy were encouraged to relate in every detail [oh I was put on group therapy to help me understand what sort of people murder kids…to help me incriminate myself] and it was always just beyond the control of the therapist, to disguise how much they were being turned on…it's just a pity WW2 ended so quickly, because then all those highly qualified nonce cases would have been gassed, instead of bringing out laws to protect them and promote their evil, plus making Freud's psychology a compulsory subject in many schools and colleges and from the way it all rapidly happened after the war, makes me wonder at times, if all those apparent jews to die in those camps, weren't converted to Judaism posthumously, being Prisoners of War from Russia, nut cases and gypsies in life.

Okay this chapter isn't just about how evil is my grandchildren's mother is… but we will get to the nitty-gritty eventually as it will prove to everyone just how evil are the laws in this god forsaken country.

Anyway after the SS discovered the fact that kids' liking me was not quite enough to make me evil, plus they had gone on line and found no evidence to support her evil hatred of me, that she cannot justify, except her excuse that whenever she gets upset, she has to hurt someone and I will always forgive her, in the hope she might start to grow up…

[Which in retrospect they should have had her committed on a NHS section and locked up in at a top security mental hospital]

So she decided to break into my house again to steal a copy of my book and then pointed out to the freaks, that my files were under the official secrets act for 75 years, which should have any normal person, either dismiss it as there is apparently no such law, plus had I been in prison and Broadmoor, I would be on all their computers and heavy conditions placed upon me…

Well having all that evidence that could have been seen as a clever story-line in a novel, she was even more determined to destroy her children's lives and my own, knowing that the best way to kill two birds with one stone, due to their unquestionable love for me and my love, that was bordering onto adoration she decided that by brainwashing the kids…that would punish me for a crime that only existed in her very sick mind, but try as I might to protect the kids, by trying to have her put away for observation…it would only take a few days for her to flip her lid, but she had the advantage of being a fantastic actress and a very convincing compulsive liar, which in part was my own fault in teaching what great fun she and her mates could have using logic, but it was too late, she was using it to destroy people's lives, especially mine if in a meeting with her in the room, she would make a wild accusation knowing I would be very embarrassed and confused, trying to figure out what she had just accused me of and my looking very guilty taken off guard, as would the kids who would plead their innocence, by demanding they also proved a negative truth, but it was worse for them as they were not allowed to question her.

Maybe I should have converted to Judaism, where everything can be proved by the postulations of paedophilia…i.e. I have a theory based on self-evidence, that everyone must accept without question and where's the evidence new born babies masturbate whilst dreaming of raping their parents…well they sleep with their hands between their legs and to a very keen eyed jew they have semi-erections… which is substantial proof and only an idiot would question such findings and they wonder why everywhere they go they are persecuted, because they always move in with perfectly healthy thinking people, who never contemplate raping their parents or children.

Not unlike that American Jew or should that be Jewish American, if there is a difference, especially when the whole world apart from those dozy Americans, knows that America is run and controlled by the jews…the point being that to weaken Iraqi's resolve not being dictated by the Zionist, the yanks put sanctions on that country, for refusing to be dictated to, by an inferior non-nation, that resulted in them putting a ban on the import of cheaply made medication, being used as a powerful weapon during the sanctions, that resulted in 200 children dying every month…but when those countries that had not put Mickey Mouse signatures to the Bill of Human Rights, pointed out that stark reality of the Jewish Americans sanctions…Madeline Albright [the harlot of Jerusalem] declared 200 innocent victims, were an acceptable number…considering the jews acts of genocide towards the Palestinians…but then she rants and raves about a few jews apparently dying in concentration camps, as an unacceptable number, plus the dozy yanks, sacrificed 160,000 of their own people, not overlooking that extra few hundred thousands of US servicemen who returned home cripples for the rest of their lives, which to Madeline was also an acceptable number, although she has never explained why at the end of WW2 more jews left Germany, than had been living in Germany before the war, but it did take a little longer than desired, for those god hating or hated countries, to create laws making it illegal to question the Zionist version of who ran the camps, plus to protect their sexual depravity, happily embraced by those inbred heads of state in Europe…

But yet again I digress…

Then my evil daughter told me, that she had discussed her version of the trial with her social worker had told her, that if she could prove more evidence, they would remove my stigma…well everyone I knew, knew about my case having found the evidence in the Lord Chancellors Office including the Forensic evidence…well everything coved in this book…so any help was welcome…but those child molesting freaks with even less evidence than I was tried on, did not put a complete ban on having contact with kids, but apparently only my grandchildren.

Oh I missed an important bit…when Lorien was about 10 years old, Ryan's father wanted to take him to Disney Land, Paris, but the mother said, only if she could go as well to which the guy [a really nice guy, not unlike all those other really nice guys who wanted to marry her, but not knowing about her con to get cash out of them] said his funding wouldn't stretch that far, suggested she got a babysitter for the weekend for Lorien and Josh, but she took that offer as a way to dump them on the freak, then spent the next couple of weeks being so psychologically evil to them, that on being told they were going back to live with him…they jumped for joy!

So I asked her why she didn't just send Josh to spend the weekend with his father and Lo to her natural father or myself, considering that for the bulk of her life she had spent every weekend with us both.

Her reply was very sick, the reason she couldn't stay with either of us was due, to both of us loving her too much, that not only would she have been very happy to stay with us, but we would have gladly taken her for however long she could stay for, plus her father had been trying for years to have her with him.

Then I pointed out everything she had been telling everyone, about his cravings for school girls and he could eventually rape her, as he had tried to do with his natural daughter, to which she almost screamed; "That's the idea, because she had always hated her!"

Sometimes I feel I am due to burn in hell for eternity, for being partly responsible for bringing such evil into the world, plus not taking all those chances to put her out of her misery, but like all those other parents of such evil freaks, I thought with love and affection she would grow out of it…

So not just for Lo's sake, but for all her kids safeties including Ryan's welfare, I contacted Lo's welfare officer, pointing out everything my daughter had been telling everyone for years and was still prepared to risk the kids safety, even if only half of it were true, but it well and truly backfired, not only did they not offer the kids protection, but it turned out the social worker was having a discreet relationship with the freak, plus ignoring the rules covering passing on the case to an independent social worker, but she took the letter straight around to the freak [who like most people without much knowledge of the written English language], hence he pointed out what my evil daughter, had told him years ago, about my case and that I should never be trusted with kids…omitting that he had hitherto been okay about letting his own kids, go out with me for weekends and holidays and had seen no reason to stop Lo staying with me, then she decided that as I had been in prison 42 years earlier or 31 years since discharge on no restrictions of movement [just never to seek for the information to clear my name in the Courts of Appeal], then on heresy along, she sentenced the kids to be denied any affection or protection, from either myself or anyone else interested in their welfare.

Plus both kids were convinced that the reasons why I had stopped seeing them, was because I hated both of them so much, that I never wanted to see them again, plus their mother supported his lies and deception…hence in a trusting and confused child's mind they swallowed it hook, line and sinker…

*   *   *   *   *

Now for a further reality of British Justice or should it be called; Even more Evidence; that The Judges that Make the Laws, condone and protect those evil freaks, that Enjoy Destroying the lives of Innocent Parents and Children!"

And Hey ho the evidence, to back up My Apparently Strange Accusations…

Well for starters, everyone that has read this far, without skipping chapters, will appreciate I am not in the habit of plagiarising, especially when the facts are on hand, regardless of the fact I was cursed at birth with a very retentive memory, that is just great when recalling truly beautiful memories, but its equal opposite for a long period of my life, almost brought about suicides, due to the precise details of my memories, that during uncontrolled sleeping dreams and at times, when thinking about things in general, I slowly drift into those times to be forgotten…which may in part help you appreciate, why it's taken so long to write this book, plus although originally to help children born with bladders that failed to disconnect at birth or as the jews would have the world believe, it's due to newly born babies wanting to rape or murder their parents…in their subconscious minds!

This section may help explain why…to quote social workers who snatch kids for snuff movies etcetera or apparently taken into care…that if the parents are innocent of the crimes thrown in the faces, then why don't they use their free rights, to appeal against the decisions of the SS.

To start with it is probably the hardest law to break apart, thanks to those child molesting judges that go out of their ways to protect social workers and nonce cases in general.

*   *   *   *   *

Unfortunately my file on the SS is missing…so to retrace my footsteps, to when I had a visit from a couple of Officials who threatened to have me incarcerated, so here I go back into the past…

I recall how they seemed to know a lot about me, due to my evil daughter not wanting me to get an extended appeal time…just so she could use logic that it's impossible to prove a negative…therefore I should not have my day in court…apart from her mother's side of the family, I have no idea why she should be so evil and a compulsive and convincing liar, plus it's not just me she hates for an unknown reason, but her mother, brother, sister, then later all her own children, to the point of dumping Lo and Josh onto a locally well-known child molester, that had tried to rape his own daughter. Add to that my computer had broken down…but although not having a computer meant all my letters were hand-written and photocopied, plus the involuntary euthanasia medication, then moving onto my boat… but although it meant writing to all the various agencies, hence the file covered all the photo copies and replies…that I hadn't looked at over the last 18 years, but when I searched for the file, it had been removed from the filling folder and replaced with poetry, I had long since convinced myself no longer exited…

But she seems to have never worked out I have a retentive memory, okay some names, times and actual dates do not come into the memories, but a lot of other things do, although it's been six months, since the last part above, searching frantically for the file that I had taken for granted was with the rest, probably due to hastily moving all my files into one big folder, when I moved onto the boat.

But there are thousands of victims of the SS that will vouch for the following, but having been through it, they will also have it branded into their memories, especially how it's impossible to get legal aid, because every legal company knows it's a waste of time, trying to get statements or replies from the SS, let alone be given the conditions for appealing against their decisions to snatch children for snuff movies, child prostitution and whatever sick reasons, that turn on their legal freaks, that the laws in this country protects.

But more recently in the wrong file, I found a letter from the Department of Education and Science, telling me my letter to the Home Office, had been passed onto them…

Then the ball started rolling in my mind, as it implies how it is possible for the SS to go into schools to snatch children that had hitherto had no reasons to be snatched, they were happy kids, no signs of physical or psychological torture, with the SS later claiming "IF" forced to explain to the public their reasons for snatching happy kids, they just say that if the victims' families or guardians are innocent, then they can always appeal against their decision, to put the child in care…whilst hap-

pily ignoring those kids, they know for a fact that their parents are mentally retarded, who are often junkies, that beat or starve their kids to death after months
of lacerations and bruising.

Now it's only a theory [or postulation], but isn't it just a little bit strange, without a history of violence against them, can be snatched from schools?

But not only snatched, but the SS has the power to get a magistrates order, to
prevent any form of the media and solicitors, from investigating their cases and
only one or two very influential families have been able to get their kids back…
minus any form of apology from those freaks.

When I contacted the DES to complain about a local SS Officer [isn't it just a
bit odd how they use the same initials as the German Gestapo, plus having so much
in common with them] I had contacted in Southend on Sea, Essex, that was my
grandchildren's social worker, plus her being a close friend of my daughters ex-hus-
band, instead of passing my letter on to a neutral investigator, decided to hush it up
herself, the DES replied it was nothing to do with them what they did in other SS
departments, implying that being the HQ of the SS has nothing to do with them,
but did send me a copy of the rules on how to appeal…a process guaranteed to take
a year or more, before getting their appeals before a judge…but wait for it…The last
condition came with the added condition; they can only go before a judge with the
permission of the SS Officer they are complaining about, with their permission…

Probably the only organisation of criminals that are exempt from justice…just
imagine what any country would be like, if rapist, murderers or just common criminals, could only be taken to court with their own permission and who brought
about this law…apart from sexually depraved judges.

Oh to return to the theory on how kids are snatched from schools, well considering the DES an SS are one and the same, plus school inspectors, may account
for how they discover which schools have the perfect candidates to be snatched to
order…mainly blonde or fair haired children…because the DES has probably got
its agents in every school, disguised as part time teachers/helpers or directors…
that are in turn protected by the laws and the police, who are not unknown to appear on nonce case websites…but then the police claim their computers were
hacked into, apparently its only the police that are found not guilty for down load-
ing child porn, whereas genuine victims of hackers have only themselves to blame.

A few years ago New Scotland Yard pointed out, that every year dozens of children's bodies are found, but could not carry out investigations as to who they were,
on the grounds that no one has reported them as missing and yes a few may have
been killed by their parents, that did not report their actions, but these kids run
into hundreds…I contacted the Commissioner of NSY to ask why they couldn't

print the faces of those victims on a missing children's website, okay it may upset the parents, but at least they won't spend the rest of their lives waiting and praying for their children to return home, but they ignored me, probably because they may discover that most of them were snatched by the SS, hence not reported to the police, who in turn may be told not to investigate the cases…

A few years ago the News of the World published a whole list with photos of child sex offenders, then some Jack the Lad had a brilliant ides, he made an anonymous phone call to their local police, imply a local nonce was about to be murdered and it worked a treat, because the police in their haste to protect them, put two coppers outside all the nonce cases homes and within hours, all the local people knew where they lived.

Back to how to appeal against an unjustifiable decision by the SS…in this instance the SS Officer was a Mss V Musters, head of Southend's SS back in 2005… first you have to write to the person directly involved in the snatching of children or protector of a child groomer, then wait a month for a reply, then write a second letter and wait another month [discounting the time to discover how to go about appealing, that isn't forthcoming unless you know exactly how to go about getting the information, maybe add a few more months], then wait again for the reply they will refuse to acknowledge, then you are expected to contact the local council director that has never been known, to question anything involving the SS and you have to constantly keep writing, until he decides to reply…that's maybe a year gone by, with your children not getting any protection, from those freaks who hate children…unless they are blonde or fair haired…and if you had put him in a line up with all the kiddie fiddlers, you would never have guessed he was not such a person, but then it is not uncommon in Southend, that whilst the councillors were in a meeting, their wives will be plying their trade in the red light district…then you have to discover who your local ombudsman is and only if he feels like it, [regardless of what the laws states] you may eventually, take your case before the children's court…and if you are extremely lucky after 2-3 years, you may be able to appeal, but only with the permission of the SS…

And to think the general public are convinced, that this country isn't controlled by nonce cases, with dozens of laws to protect them and extremely few to protect children, especially in the care of the SS!

But then my evil daughter pointed out I had been in prison, plus I have a strange power, that causes children to like me for no apparent reason whatsoever [in her twisted mind], then without any knowledge of the case and an outright refusal to look at any evidence…including why my name has never appeared on their computers [not just as a threat, but not even an implied possible case of concern to the authorities], so my evil daughter stole even more evidence, that were part of my grounds for an appeal 40 years after the event took place, without any forensic evidence to imply I was remotely involved in the crime…but a Zionist Nazi promoter of unquestionable theories, based upon self-evidence, decided that anyone who was still incontinent at 16 years of age, are obviously a psychopath and likely to turn into a schizophrenic, regardless of there being no evidence of psychopaths or schizophrenics suffering from incontinence…which must also help psychiatrist reach any conclusion they fantasize about whilst masturbating, knowing the courts will never question an expert nonce promoter, plus his evidence will be protected under the "Official Secrets Act", until 25 years after their death.

I sometimes wonder how many child molesters, rapist or infanticides are being protected, under the Best Justice System in the World…namely British Justice… where the laws are made by the Judges, to Protect the Judges and those perverts that are supposed to protect everyone and especially young children, without immunity given to those guilty Zionist psychologists who claim it is perfectly natural for children to want to rape or be raped by their parents in their subconscious minds and it is everyone's duty to promote their children's desires, based on the twisted translation of a sexually depraved Zionist psychologist, who had translated 13 lines of a tragic Greek play [that is in 3 parts] and based on purely mythical characters, whilst ignoring the stories of Lot and his daughters or any number of events in jewish history, in which the entire tribe is wiped out , except for a brother and sister or parent and child, that then went out to create a new jewish tribe…according to their scriptures.

It's a toss-up in this country as to which is the more serious crimes and their punishments, between not paying parking fines or raping their own children or the even worse cases of a parent beating up a pervert, that has raped their child, plus by attacking them, the judges say; they have been punished enough and throw the cases out of court, to reassure the rapist that they are free to continue raping children and hope they only get a punch on the nose!

Rapist in general and let alone how many child molesters that do go into our prisons are given special privileges and protection, from common criminals, plus massive reductions in their sentences, because they are not considered to be criminals, but very misunderstood people, that are also protected due to their Human Rights, those same rights they refused to give to their victims, the rights not to become victims.

But then those freaks may point out, that if a law hadn't come into being, in which psychologically disturbed people cannot be punished…I in turn would never have been cured of incontinence that turned out to be a physical reality, rather than a sick postulation in the twisted minds of those in the medical profession and not just in my mind.

Yep I will admit there are times when I wish I had never had never been cured, because it helped destroy my life and the lives of my grandchildren, but hey it is great being able to go out on cold days, without the urgent need to repeatedly finding somewhere to urinate, stay overnight at friends' houses or take breaks in hotels and guest houses and start living the life most people take for granted, but because I was asked to write this story in the hope of protecting the futures of other equally innocent children, suffering with a bladder that failed to disconnect at birth.

* * * * *

Chapter 7
Lorien

Recently [it's now 2007] with the help of your Evil Mother and equally as Evil Step Father, that between themselves managed to brainwash your mind, into accepting that the only person [namely myself] that Loved and at times Adored You, now hated you so much that I never wanted to see you again and to prove their point, pointed out how I never came to see you anymore.

Then when you escaped the clutches of the freak and ran to your mother for protection, you were rejected and convinced, that you would be wasting your time trying to find me, because everyone hates you…to the point you attempted suicide, much to everyone's delight except mine.

I tried repeatedly to find out where you were, even after that evil e-mail with a blocked reply added, I still searched for you, by phoning all the mental hospitals and hostels to discover where you were, in the hope of being able to help you to recover and hopefully give me a good reason to be happy again, before I die, but even the psychiatric units I discovered are run by freaks, who kept giving me numbers to contact, that in turn sent me back to them, then they decided that the only people allowed to contact you were your parents, but if you wanted to contact me you will phone me, when I asked them to give you my phone number, they refused to pass it on…in fact refused to take it down on paper, because I am only your Grandfather or could it have been, because lonely 16 year old girls, can be great sport if they have no one to complain to.

But those sick and evil freaks [your parents] did not tell you that they had social services help, to prevent me from having any contact with you or your siblings on the flimsy grounds, that I have a strange power over kids [and adults] that causes them to like and trust me for no reason whatsoever…in their limited imaginations that have no concept of self-respect, nonsexual Love or Compassion towards vulnerable children, that are very trusting…

Then I found myself analysing the concept of loneliness that everyone goes through in their lives at various degrees, the most common is caused by waiting for someone to show up for a meal or going somewhere that would make you both happy, but then they can't be bothered to either turn up or making a phone call to explain they can't make it.

So a person ends up thinking they are a bit late, then very late and not knowing what to do if convinced they are on their way, thereby trapping you in your house, still convinced they will show up and no means of contacting them, as the walls slowly start to shrink and claustrophobia fills in the vacuums between both your mind or worse still, if it in your heart and is a very special friend.

Thinking back to those times years ago, when the most soul destroying situations were caused by anticipation, knowing without a doubt that the person you have absolute trust in and has never let you down…doesn't bother to turn up or make a call.

A bit like years ago having made some great plans for a fun day, then something turns up that scuppers all the plans, especially if they were kids…so at the first possible moment I would phone them or pop around [in those days before everyone had a phone, let alone a mobile phone] to explain the situation and stupid or very vague parents would say, don't worry the kids will forget they were supposed to having a great day/weekend out, but reflecting back over my life in the Homes, when people convinced me they will give me a great day out or a short holiday, only to never be seen again, but then with those memories in my mind, there was no way I would do that to anyone else, so I would ask the parent to put the kid on the phone for a chat and to cover my embarrassment [okay I will admit that occasionally, when a person has repeatedly not been bothered to turn up or make a call, I would make plans for a venue, I knew they would really enjoy…then disappear for the weekend, without telling anyone, so they can have a practical experience of what their contempt causes to others]…

Anyway with kids [after a slight moan]they were willing to forgive me, because it turned out to be a great novelty that someone had phoned "Them" and would brag to all their friends, that someone had phoned them, plus the adults were appreciative, because it gave them time to make other plans.

Although there are a lot of people who seem to confuse loneliness with being on your own, as one and the same thing…I have spent most of my life being on my own, due in part to having severe incontinence [that sometimes when musing to myself , as to why I hadn't done this or that years ago, having over these last 20 odd years, forgotten I had once been severely incontinent…unless a situation arises when it's important to remember, especially when trying to help someone in the same situation, but for the most part, would rather not get involved, due to the depressions such memories conjure up and the added sadness caused by having a retentive memory, that blurs what happened years ago and today, that in turn causes another form of loneliness, because there is no immediate way to communicate with anyone else, that can appreciate the reason for being so depressed and yeah maybe the easier option for people incapable of self-analysis is to commit suicide.

It's a bit like being in prison, for me it was just an extension of being on my own, whereas people who have fond memories of their families or their kids growing up and not being there to share those experiences, but then they deserve the added punishment, due to not taking such things into consideration when trying to impress everyone they are a Jack the Lad…in fact the number of times a lot of people constantly return to prison, may be due to feeling important in a close knit society, whereas on civvy street they are merely treated with a deserved contempt.

Then there are the people who allow themselves to become depressed after the lights go out, because they have nothing to distract them, then there are those who refuse to be isolated and just let their bodies be in prison, whilst their minds are free to roam, especially those who have learnt to meditate and it doesn't matter if they are put into solitary confinement, they are never or very rarely become part of the situation…and yeah before learning how to meditate, I use to fall asleep crying and during social periods, pretending I did not give a damn one way or another, but rarely felt loneliness…plus having a shortwave radio was a great distraction… which was just a state of mind or so I thought, until Lorien and Ryan were taken out of my life, because I had taken it for granted, they will always be there and the adventures I had had with their mother when she was their age and the other kids who came along for a day out or long weekend, but then my relationship with Lorien was more than just special, because she knew long before me, that I would be coming to see her, long before it entered my mind to visit on the spur of the moment and our most common bond between us being unquestionable love and very much unlike her mother, there were never any preconditions that expected rewards on top of a special treat, like going on holidays, but only on her conditions…

Damn it this maybe the start of another mild depression and just like the last year or so…I haven't gone anywhere near this chapter, although it may have helped if someone had shown me how to get each chapter in its right sequence, rather than finding it, printing out a copy, then with one finger typing it all out again, yeah I know they do manuals…that are useless if you don't understand all the jargon, that has replaced English from my era, but the main reason for avoiding it [like so many other chapters that eventually were erased] is the feelings of great loss and loneliness, in part due to having had so many great dreams for the future with Lo and

Ryan and never thought for one moment of how far her evil mother would go to destroy her life…which should have never happened, considering she had myself and her natural father to turn to for unquestionable love and affection, but then if they put him through, the same as they did to me by getting his access to keep in touch with her via the SS and what makes it worse was how her evil mother, gladly sent Lo to live with a freak that would probably rape her, due to his insatiable lust for school girls including his own daughter.

The worst part is not knowing if she is dead or alive and no way of contacting her, which as that evil e-mail she sent to me, with a blocked return…she has been completely convinced that her evil mother, was telling her the truth about how much I hate her and I was the reason everyone else hates her too, but I have no idea who any of her friends are or how to contact them, to open her eyes to the truth.

But then if she has turned out to be anything like her mother, grandmother and great grandmother, I would be better off not bothering to seek or find her, but I cannot rid myself of all those beautiful memories of when we were together and her strange gift of just knowing, I was coming to see her, long before I knew myself or when pretending to fall asleep, to get her to sleep, then opening my eyes, discovering we had both slept all night…except her first 11 years, she was nothing like her mother and all those other women on her side of the family, plus we just enjoyed being together and I have no idea how many times it would take an hour or more to remember we hadn't greeted each other as normal people do when meeting up…it was usually myself that would ask; "Have we forgotten anything?" Then she would frown, deep in thought before throwing her arms around me, planting a kiss on my cheek and telling me how much she loved me, as I apologised for forgetting as well, but hey when did love require words, except on cards and gifts…

Yet in retrospect a lot of what took place between Lo's mother and myself, may have never come about, if I hadn't always given her another chance to become mature instead or giving her physical punishments, that on the very few occasions I did lose it, she became very affectionate towards me, but I didn't like the idea of having to beat her into submission or anyone else come to that, but hey in many ways the old adage may contain a lot of really, that to spare the rod will destroy the kid, but then there are a lot of freaks around, who cannot differentiate between a short sharp punishment and deriving sexual enjoyment from beating up on defenceless kids, because a lot of people are violent just for the sake of it, a bit like those kids who join the military for adventure, then have to be taught how to kill people and I have no idea how many times I almost reached the stage of killing her, but instead kept changing my mind or finding an excuse not to find a psychopath who likes beating people up in public places, for the sheer joy of it, then offering them a victim who justified being beaten for a bit of rumination and hope they don't take it out on me for being the only witness or becoming a victim of blackmail [whilst overlooking, that in not doing so…she would destroy the lives of so many people. Especially her own children and family…if we had lived in the USA such a problem would have been easily solved with their gun laws…But now it is too late, I am old, weaker in body that has obtained so many disabilities, to be a psychical threat to anyone, plus almost forgotten memories of being in Broadmoor that will never be related and the chances are I may still be in better health [not overlooking those years of having an ulcer and refused treatment, unless I was prepared to make the authorities happy…but then maybe life would have been better in so far as things may have been different on a second visit to there, because I would have been guilty of an actual crime and have my human rights recognised…and all my ailments taken care of, but now I have had experiences of life, that didn't exist when I was there, but then I wasn't on drugs and apparent suicides were not investigated and all those accursed memories, may have ended years ago…but I still need to find Lo and if she has been killed, like a lot of young girls in psychiatric hospitals on day or weekend release that are seen walking arm in arm laughing and very happy, before apparently going to the top floors of flats or multistoried car parks and then jumping to their deaths or murdered by the staff, who will happily frame a patient high on drugs, that is very naïve and almost illiterate, with no idea what is going on and happily help the police with their enquires, until they are framed with murder and end up in a top security hospital, that to them is just another hospital etcetera…and who knows if eventually when the drugs start wearing off, find they have no memories of having killed anyone and when pointing this out to their doctors, they either get offered a deal, to incriminate themselves, to keep the records clean [or die in their sleep] before eventually being discharged and start having nervous breakdowns, because they cannot communicate with anyone and drift into loneliness, whilst everyone else seems to be enjoying life. Plus the only people who offer to help just rip them off or worse…

Plus the answer to the question as to why young teenagers in such institutions are not allowed to communicate with anyone, other than those responsible for their states of mind in the first place, just what sort of freaks enjoy convincing kids that everyone hates them, especially those that do love them, but are banned from having any reassuring contact with them, because they are not immediate family, including grandparents or their siblings, that the nut house convince them, that the patient doesn't want to see them or make contact…it's as if my own life is repeating itself in many ways, my own lifetime and in my Lo's 53 years later, if for completely different reasons…it is obviously long overdue to build gas chambers to rid the world of those freaks, going under the guises of doctors and nurses, when in reality they are sexually depraved freaks wasting the earth limited resources and its oxygen.

I once met a woman in Runwell Essex, who had spent 20 years in that nut house, after she had a nervous breakdown, cause by her husband and baby being killed in a car accident, but instead of giving her a mild tonic and definitely no compassion, they put her on a severe anti-depressant that had more than a dozen side effects...that in turn required more medication to counteract, the first heavy dosage of drugs, with protection from the NHS, with MP's not being interested in their plight, because such people do not vote.

A bit like the Urispas I was put on for three times a day, but in too many ways over the years had almost lost all hope in the No Help Service [NHS], so started by taking one a day, which in turn could have killed me, except The Fates were smiling on me gently and sent momentarily into my life a registered nurse who took me to the reference section of the local library...at which point I stopped taking them, without too many serious side-effects, due to , the best side effects caused forgetfulness which also caused me to stop taking them, plus the best side effect being exactly the same as being stoned, plus having lost everything during that period, including several insurance policies and shares, my home and various side effects that prevented me from working, therefore my company...Hence over the next two years, whenever I had to report to the clinic or DHS, I would smoke a joint and turn up apparently with all the symptoms, but the experts couldn't figure out, why I was still alive, considering I was apparently taking 21 pills a week [or 84 a month] plus had been on them for a couple of years, before buying an old boat and gave up on the NHS, but then it took well over 8 years to almost overcome all the side effects.

It often causes me to wonder why the pharmaceutical companies are allowed to create drugs, that are designed to kill people, that are rarely ill prior to being yet another victim of involuntary euthanasia and yet will not prescribe them to the terminally ill or in great physical pain...unless being compassionate doesn't turn them on sexually, plus how much of those company profits, go into the over bulging wallets of GP's, for prescribing the drugs and thinking back...none of those drugs came with any literature on such things as side effects...the patient just gets told, they have no side effects whatsoever...thus the local chemist must be in on the plot to legally murder patients, maybe I was just a lousy patient that they rarely saw, from year to year and took note of what was good or bad and whether or not they could be bought over the counter...not only that, but how many older people [I was only 47/8 when prescribed them and in almost perfect health]bother to read the side effects, without wearing powerful reading glasses plus a strong magnifying glass.

I have over the past few years been given drugs, that after as little as two doses, either caused diarrhoea or severe depressions…one I refused to take, because being very weak on my legs, I will never reach the toilet in time, resulting in constantly changing my underwear, plus my flat would stink of excrement and a great put off for any visitors…unless actively gay for whom it would appear, the stench of human excrement is not only a big turn on, but drives them past the point of wanting to impale themselves into it.

Not unlike years ago in prison, if they wanted someone sectioning they would put them in a padded cell and add very strong laxatives to their food and refused to let them use the toilet, back in the days when toilets were not in cells, but had to use chamber pots…[although come to think about it, I doubt if they would put a toilet in a padded cell], then a week later bring in an independent and very gullible GP to examine them…no words were exchanged…between them, because the moment they opened the hatch, the stench in the cell was so bad, the GP would just sign the documents, no questions asked and within a few days they were off to a top security funny farm with no date for discharge…they did more or less the same with me, except in my case it was my teeth, that were causing me to "act strangely"… that were a few days later taken out by a mobile dental surgery, given a few weeks to recover, then put on the magic bus to Broadmoor.

Another pill I was given the prescription for…before having time to sit down, let alone not asked what was ailing me, whose most common side effect was severe depressions…well never having met anyone who was so deliriously happy…that they required a pill to help them experience severe depressions, although it should be prescribed as a compulsory drug to be taken by GP's and funny farm workers, [three times a day for a week] to help them communicate with severely depressed patients, if they survive all the temptations to commit suicide, with countless means to succeed, starting with everyone studying Freudian psychology, that helps them communicate with another person's subconscious, via theories based on self-evidence…that shall never be questioned, in case reality proves otherwise, so I took the pills back to the chemist to dispose of…okay I took two, the first gave me a state of being stoned, hence needless to say I was looking forward to the second dose, but that caused me to pass out and woke up severely depressed and almost suicidal…then did what I had overlooked doing in the first place…I read the side effects and discovered the most common side effect was severe depressions…but why prescribe them or worse still, why do the pharmaceutical companies make them, let alone bribe GP's to prescribe them, whilst knowing full well their victims will more than probably commit suicide [yeah it may be a ploy to dispose of all the white English people in this country, excluding GP's and Government Ministers who will move to the luxurious apartments around the world, due to their very high salaries for doing nothing, but kill innocent people, not that successive governments have not sent hundreds of our military personnel, to die bravely in wars that have nothing to do with this country, that hasn't had war declare on them] plus if a person commits suicide all the insurance companies are happy, not having to pay up on the policies or if their relations are stupid enough to have them put under "expert" supervision, where they get more powerful drugs to control, what could turn out to make the first anti-depressants seem very mild…

Needless to say I don't visit them anymore, regardless of the pains wracking through my body and praying I will survive long enough to get this finished before dying, in the vague hope that I will not be reincarnated and as a further punishment, be forced to live this life over again and gawd knows what crime I had been guilty of in my previous life…probably a pope or Sigmund Freud or not having solved the problem of kids being born with bladders that failed to open properly at birth, well probably could have but couldn't be bothered…but then if I could learn to type when stoned…I wouldn't keep wandering off to seek distractions from these mild depressions, that can escalate out of all depressions, but hey being nice for the hell of it, works okay…sometimes.

Oh looking back at the last paragraph…I am not recommending people smoking or cooking pot whilst depressed, because in those cases [just like alcohol] it can make your situation worse and here I am digressing from another digression and on top of that I have written this chapter and a few more already, but cannot figure out how to insert them back into this folder, having wandered off, when clicking "save" and another thing I can claim to be…is "a lousy copy typist"…hence even more digressions, wander into my mind, then into print.

I sometimes feel the worse causes of loneliness's are the same as being very devoutly in love with someone for years, then one partner dying…which oddly enough seems to affect more men than women, when it's taken into consideration, that when old ladies die, it's not uncommon for the guy to quickly follow from a broken heart and utter loss, but on the other hand when the husband dies first… especially if well insured, their wives carry on for years having a good time, we have some women in this complex, whose husbands died 20 to 30 years ago.

But with me [if I let it get out of hand] my loneliness has been losing all contact with Lo and Ryan, after years of dreams of the great fun we were going to have together visiting the countryside, old castles, museums and galleries and helping them understand how beautiful our natural country is and not forgetting the lakes and mountains, but somewhere along the way, I had forgotten or overlooked just how evil their mother was/is, plus it's a bit confusing, because on the one hand I love them both, with the same intensity as their mother hates them and everyone else directly related to her, especially her brother Paul who she managed to get a court ruling that he cannot go to Southend to visit anyone in his family, after he was trapped by his evil sister, into hitting her after months of violence from her…for no known reason, except maybe he was an easy target and eventually hit her the once and was all but charged with attempted murder, after she went to the police with her well-practiced tears and perfected terror…the poor guy is even more timid than I was at his age, plus the negative response from his mother, whenever his sister implied he was guilty of whatever she wanted him to be guilty of, as if she spent her entire childhood practicing being evil, including attacking or bullying the little kids that lived on her estate, then claiming she was the victim and everyone believed her…I caught her a couple of times beating up on little Karen and when I demanded to know why, she would just say, that whenever she gets upset, she has to attack and hurt somebody…

If Lo is still alive I am just hoping she will not fall into the trap most hated [by their evil parents] kids fall into, by trying to win their parents love or with Lo… wasting her life thinking she was to blame for her mother's evil towards her, because all she will ever get will be contempt until the day her mother dies, which may be a long time into the future, because really selfish and evil women live for a long time and then only to destroy people's lives, a bit like my father confessing on his death bed, that every time he realized a woman was in love with me, he would tell them very convincing lies to scare them away, in case I left him on his own…fortunately the best thing he ever did, was to die before I had time to kill the lousy bastard…having enjoyed his own life and had been married twice and it was only just before he died, I realized he had been ripping me off with tales of woe, a bit like whenever it was obvious I was planning a weekend break, having on too many occasions having done so over the years…he would end up at deaths door…until it was too late to travel, then he would have a miraculous recovery and go off to the club with his mates, until eventually I just went and told him about my great weekend away, on getting home…but the funny bit being, that when he was actually dying, I just took it as another con on its way and probably the last thing he heard, was my laughing at him after years of being at deaths door…but then it was taken for granted by the nurses, that I was aware of the situation without anyone telling me anything…a bit like yelling at drivers who do one signal, then do the complete opposite…that results in my yelling; "Hey I am supposed to be a psychopath , not a bleeding telepath!" so he died with me laughing, after years of crying wolf.

But after almost a whole life time of being on my own except for when doing charity work and sometimes, having something to look forward to the next day, all I have left after those years on and off this book, is hopefully having helped an as yet to be born kid, with a bladder that fails to open correctly and not knowing my own experiences as its own…a bit like planting trees I will never see again, but hope they will outlive me and my only sadness is in not seeing Lo and Ryan again or if Lo is still alive, but hey who knows I may be reincarnated as one of her children and half hoping she doesn't turn out like her evil mother, grandmother and great grandmother…which yeah is a lot to hope for…

Of course this book may upset a few people, especially those who repeatedly tell me, I should face up to reality, instead of being a too well laid back hippie and to get a life…well that has been my life and what do you consider your reality as, probably they were just normal people, who obey the rules and never questioned anything, especially not those self-appointed bastions of society, that decide how everyone should respect their postulations of being their superiors, whilst in private they are molesting children…

Maybe loneliness has nothing to do with being alone, but being alone in an empty world and hoping that deep void between myself and my grandchildren … and Lo don't feel too guilty about your email, because it was obvious the words were those of your mother, to help even further to keep us apart, but it would be nice to meet you and say; "Have You Forgotten anything Lorien?"

ALMOST THE END

Now to summarise;

I suppose in many ways I am guilty and being punished severely for overlooking a very important knowledge, I had gained over the years, but the happiness of having Lo and Ryan in my life caused me to forget, that every good experience is followed by a negative, but just as powerful experience.

Years ago I wrote out a long beautiful love poem…forgotten what it was called, but it ended with the line; "I want to Love You, but I have become so afraid of Love!" oh it had nothing to do with my early childhood and youth, but falling too deeply in love with a beautiful woman and it all going wrong…

Oh I do have other grandchildren, but no idea how many although there was a girl who would be sent into her bedroom when I arrived, but always seemed to be happy enough when I took them all out for lunch, but she was not around at weekend, because from being a few days old…onwards she was always at her father's and paternal grandparents house from Friday pm until Monday am, plus if her father hadn't been so dozy, with well-heeled parents, the chances are she wouldn't have spoken to him, let alone dragged him to her bedroom, until she was certain she had conceived, then bye bye Mr Nice-Guy, but still a source of a steady income, for her to go out clubbing, but I rarely saw her parents and on those rare occasions we bumped into each other and treated me with contempt, due probably due to my evil daughter feeding them the line, that I was a paedophile and she is such a convincing liar, plus they were so dozy they never questioned her, that if that was the case, then why did she let Lo and Ryan stay with me every other weekend on my boat, if I was such an evil threat to children, but then I should I suppose give my daughter some credit, for not only finding Muppets, but also well-heeled Muppets.

Then there is Ryan whose father would visit him occasionally with gifts, but not to pay for her to go clubbing, but then she did wangle a trip to Disney Land Paris out of him, plus used the occasion to dump Lo onto the freak ...along with Josh who is just weird and if he couldn't have all the attention, he would go and hide, then deliberately crap himself...I caught him straining a couple of times and dragged him off to the toilet, but then he is the freaks natural son, so it must be in his DNA...his other problem made him a bit scary to take out anywhere, on a one to one basis, because the moment I let go of his hand, he would just vanish and the last time we were together was on the End of Southend Pier, that was deserted and I was convinced he had fallen through the railings, but it turned out he had run off to the gift shop, we had been watching a tall ship sailing by under full sail and I was chatting away to him until I looked down and he was gone.

Just before Ryan was born, Lo and Josh had been sent to live with the freak, before knowing his reputation for school girls, but at the same time recalling how it had taken quite some time to convince Martin and Emma [his own kids] that it was okay to smile...even longer to get them to laugh out loud, by taking them on picnic's or to the boat for weekends, until eventually camping with the blind, they were starting to make friends in the area and at school, plus when he started interfering with Emma, gave her the courage to run to her grans home...but then she found it very funny when Lo had tried to commit suicide, because between the freak and her evil mother, she was convinced nobody liked her and I was the cause of all the hatred in her direction.

But I was so happy seeing Lo every Friday night, sharing a meal, reading her stories and having a bath, plus he did my washing...I had completely forgotten how terrified his own kids had been, when I first met them. ..and it had been a long time since I last saw their evil mother.

Then one day visiting a friends flat, discovered she had moved in downstairs and met Ryan, within whom I fell instantly in love with...he was the same as Lo... that bond that appears between grandparents and the baby [yeah and well-adjusted

parents] where love is instant and without anything other than a spiritual bond…
he used to call me; dad dad, pointing to his father saying dad, then pointing at myself and saying dad dad, which was great child logic…then his evil mother went to
the freak to boost I had started seeing her again, which was far from the truth, I
only saw her to have access to Ryan.

The following Friday the freak gave me the ultimatum that I stopped seeing
my daughter or stop seeing Lo and being a control freak he would not listen to reason…no wonder he was the darling of Social Services and it's a wonder they didn't
make him a social worker , having all the right qualifications to destroy families…

Hence I was banned from his house, which is where I started to overlook the
yin and the yang, hence from then on I only saw Lo every other weekend at her
mother's flat and then she kept hiding from me or refused to speak to me, which
really upset me, because I loved her so very much, then not being able to control
my emotions, I demanded of her to explain why and she told me it was because I
hated her so much, that I never wanted to see her again and never wanted her to
see the dogs [she adored] on my boat…

What a sick freak, taking it out on a naïve and trusting child, because I would
not let myself be controlled by him, because his ex-wife had dumped him, when
she discovered she had become too old for him to control and kept beating him
up, whenever she came home to find a school girl with him and his obsession
with them…anyway I told Lo and the others to put on their shoes and coats and
off we went to have a picnic on the boat…her mother took a photo of the sheer
joy on her face, as she embraced me and its now just one of the two photos of her
I keep on display, but sadly enough, just looking at them causes me a lot of anguish and depressions.

But at those times I was happy just having Lo and Ryan in my life, then that
evil bitch after getting control for Lo [and her weird brother Joshua] to live with
her, sent them back to the freak, because she wanted to go to Disney Land with
Ryan's father, but I still kept popping in to see Ryan, before being hit with another
bomb shell, because he started crying whenever we met, asking why I never wanted
to take him out anymore or stay with me on my boat, so I asked his evil mother
the same question, to which she replied, she had had my name put on the child
protection register on the grounds that I have a strange power over children, that
caused them to like me for no apparent reason, thus being a threat to children and
from then on I have been banned from seeing any of my grandchildren and if I saw
them again, she would have me arrested …then a few weeks later she asked if I still
loved her, to which I replied; "Only as much as she loved her own children!" We
have never spoken since!"

I spent 11 years of unquestionable happiness with Lo and a lot of years with Ryan and since my last visit to Ryan, living in loneliness, as if as a punishment for loving them almost like deities, but forgot that every positive reality has an equally negative reality, with no desire to be happy again without my two grandchildren being a special part of my life, but secretly live in hope of being with them again, but sadly they may have been totally brainwashed into intensely hating me and it is probable it all started, when I offered a vulnerable pregnant girl a bit of compassion, that came from a long line of women, with a history of destroying people's lives, when I was being nice for the hell of it [giving a practical damn about them and if life has taught me anything, then it's to dump evil kids as quickly as possible and not making excuses for their evil, because the only reward on offer, will be a life of utter loneliness, whilst waiting for death to take me into its arms to give me compassion.

*   *   *   *   *

So that is it my friends…looking back over life most of it was crap, but hey on the bright side I have had a better life than a lot of people, who just cannot be bothered to go anywhere or do anything other than visit the pub or follow the crowd to sporting events or local fireworks displays, plus a lot of kids of my time [and since] had been mercifully killed and others never figured out how to come to terms with their experiences and committed suicide…not that I couldn't write a chapter on how not to kill yourself or should that be…something always went wrong, no matter what precautions were taken, not to be found until too late and end up as a zombie in a nut house or completely paralysed and incapable of escaping from their unwanted lives, that had been far better than what they have now…some people and kids die accidentally from a knock on their head, whereas people like me, who were battered unconscious almost every day, with lumps of wood, high heeled shoes, leather belts or attacked with knives…all now just memories of a time to be forgotten…that return to haunt me, when I consider beating up on defenceless people, using that sick joke, "Well that's the way I was treated, so it's all I know!" Utter bullshit of nonce cases and their promoters!

Yet I figured out how to avoid a lot of memories from returning, via distractions…when I know they are returning, either by being nice for the hell of it or running away to cry alone, then come back, with my face covered in smiles, as if nothing negative has ever taken place in my life, okay it's not an easy thing to do and yep I also managed to scare a few people at night, when I couldn't prevent some of those memories, from visiting me in my sleep or drifting into memories of my grandchildren and my evil daughter.

Okay I admit I went through a lot of pain before my operation, by tying things too tight to prevent myself being taken short, then reflect on all those beautiful places, people only ever see, when pulling into layby's or clearings and greeted with a beautiful vista, most of which are now motorways or by-passes and always pretending I don't have a care in the world and have absolutely no idea about facing up to reality…but then were those morons basing my experiences on what their own limitations on life…therefore so should be everyone else's, but then they will never figure out, that making people really happy, will be returned to you as genuine happiness, regardless how phoney your original happiness had been…it's really easy to be nice…try it sometime, you may be amazed that…Simplicity is the infinite truth, behind ineffable beauty and if it wasn't for an ugly cloud, we would never have beautiful sunrises or sunsets and if I wasn't framed and sent to prison, I would probably be the village idiot right now and none of this could have ever been written and who knows how much shit will be hitting the fan in government departments, as they frantically try to do yet another cover up and never envisaged the World Wide Web would be beyond their control.

Oh well cheerio and May the Joys of Peace and Love, grow as Ineffably Beautiful Flowers, Along All the Roads of Your Lives

Greck Thewandera

*　　　*　　　*　　　*　　　*

So that it folks, the reason for appearing to be too laid back and never facing up to reality, until now and to end this I will search out a poem, written on the beach on my first weekend in society, that became a favourite of Ronald Pratt QC, who found it almost impossible to accept it was written the first day I was almost free, but then freedom is just an illusion, because it means living without fear and having to live with the fear of being returned to Broadmoor on a postulation of a psychology that as with Freud's Electra, seeking revenge via justice, is merely a form of sexual depravity…anyone with the half a brain to accept without question psychology or should that be; Has anyone ever accepted the postulations of psychology, without trying to justify their depraved sexual desires towards their parents and children…

Requiem To A Seagull

I found you there on the beach,
Naked of flesh

And torment straining your dead face.
Where had you come from?
Only to be washed up on Westcliffe's shore.

Children rolling in the sand ignore you
You the once graceful ghost
Of a long ago drowned sailor.
You!
Who soared the tidal breezes
Yet stayed motionless in gale force winds.
The dogs even ignore you now
Your splendor and serenity lost forever
A million stones beneath you
But none bury you.

Old woman in a deck chair
Listens to Spartacus on a battered radio.
Cars rush by spewing pollution
Thinned by the air currents off the Thames.

The tide far out on a forgotten horizon
Just You and I
I who look and wonder
Just why we should meet in your desolation

I was enjoying my walk
But maybe seeing you
Will help me appreciate
The tides of life!

Greck, January 1975.